# NORTH BY NORTHWEST

# NORTH BY NORTHWEST

# NORTH BY NORTHWEST
## Ernest Lehman

*faber and faber*

First published in 1999
by Faber and Faber Limited
3 Queen Square London WC1N 3AU

This edition is for promotional purposes only
Not for resale

Photoset by Parker Typesetting Service, Leicester
Printed in Great Britain by
Mackays of Chatham plc, Chatham, Kent

Ernest Lehman is hereby identified as author of this
work in accordance with Section 77 of the
Copyright, Designs and Patents Act 1988

A CIP record for this book
is available from the British Library

ISBN 0-571-20564-X

2 4 6 8 10 9 7 5 3 1

# CONTENTS

Introduction, vii

## NORTH BY NORTHWEST, I

Ernest Lehman, Eva Marie Saint and Alfred Hitchcock.

# INTRODUCTION

In movie theaters and on television sets around the world, it seems as though *North by Northwest* will go on for ever. Forty-some-odd years ago, it seemed to me that *writing* that film would go on for ever, too. Actually, it took me a year.

Composer Bernard Herrmann had brought Alfred Hitchcock and me together for lunch one day because Benny thought the two of us would get along rather well. We did, and after lunch, I stood happily beside Hitch watching him shoot scenes for *Rear Window* at Paramount. Soon after, he requested, through our mutual agent, that I write the screenplay for *The Wreck of the Mary Deare* at MGM, who had bought the novel for him.

I couldn't see a movie in it. I turned him down.

Hitch was furious, I was told.

Our mutual agent then talked him (and me) into having lunch at the Polo Lounge of the Beverly Hills Hotel. We had such a good time together that I agreed to do *Mary Deare*. But after three weeks of beating-around-the-bush story conferences at his Bel Air home, I arrived one morning and said, 'I have bad news for you, Hitch. I don't know how to do this picture. You'll have to get yourself another writer.'

'Don't be silly,' he said calmly. 'We get along so well. We'll do something else instead.'

'But what'll we tell Metro?' I said.

'We won't tell them,' he replied, straight-faced.

'Something else' became two months of back-and-forth ping-ponging of ideas, some of them good, but not for me. One day I said, 'All I want to do is write the Hitchcock picture to end all Hitchcock pictures.'

'And what would that be?' he enquired.

I shrugged. 'Something with wit, glamor, sophistication, suspense, many different colorful locals, a real movie movie.'

He said nothing for a while. Then he murmured wistfully, 'I always wanted to do a chase across the faces of Mount Rushmore.'

'Hey!' I exclaimed, straightening up in my chair.

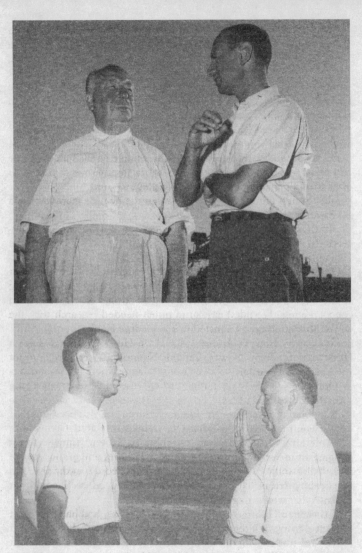

Hitchcock and Lehman in the broiling sun of Bakersfield, California, discussing camera angles for the crop-duster sequence.

There followed many weeks in which we tried to figure out who was chasing whom, and why. Meanwhile, Hitch had to devote a good deal of his attention to a little something he was preparing called *Vertigo*. I alternated between phoning him and asking for more meetings, and phoning my agent and telling him to get me off this impossible project. 'You can't quit,' my agent said. 'You already quit once. Get back to work.'

Hitch was much more helpful. 'I always wanted to do a scene,' he said one day, 'where our hero is standing all alone in a wide open space and there's nobody and nothing else in sight for three hundred and sixty degrees around, as far as the eye can see . . . and then along comes a tornado. No place to run.'

'But wait a minute,' I said. 'How can the heavies manufacture a *tornado*?'

Thus was the crop-duster sequence born, acted out, shot-by-shot, by Hitch and me in the living-room of his home. I played the plane. He played the diesel truck.

I hammered out a partial outline. Hitch informed the front office what I was up to. The executives were delighted, assuming they'd get two Hitchcock pictures instead of one. Hitch went off to shoot *Vertigo*. I headed east on a much-needed research trip: the adventures of Roger Thornhill, a.k.a. George Kaplin.

First stop, New York City – the Plaza Hotel. Where to stage a kidnapping? Then to the United Nations. Where to commit murder? Then to Glen Cove, Long Island, where I persuaded a cooperative judge to put me through the experience of being arrested for drunk driving. I took the *Twentieth Century Limited* to Chicago (but never met an 'Eve'), explored the Ambassador East Hotel, covered a Chicago auction, trained to Rapid City, South Dakota, stayed at the Sheraton Johnson Hotel, hired a forest ranger on his weekend off, and started climbing one of the faces of Mount Rushmore. Halfway to the top, I looked down dizzily. 'I'm a screenwriter. What am I doing up here?' I cried. 'I could get killed!'

I clambered down, bought a Polaroid camera, and had the forest ranger photograph the entire top of the monument. It turned out there was no place up there for a scene. (Later, the US Department of National Park refused to allow Hitch to shoot at Mount Rushmore, and the United Nations said no, too. No problem.

Gifted production designer Robert Boyle created the amazing Faces of the Presidents on the sound stages of MGM, and his magical sets also gave the film Vandamm's getaway house near the monument and the interior of the United Nations, as well.)

Now I had nothing left to do, no place else to go, no time left to stall, so I returned to California and started the endless task of writing a screenplay in my lonely office #206, the Thalberg Building, MGM, while Hitch finished *Vertigo* and took a desperately needed vacation in the British West Indies.

I mailed the first half of my work to him and received a cheerful, cheering four-page hand-written letter from Round Hill Hotel, Montego Bay, Jamaica. 'My dear Ernie . . . Let me say how much I enjoyed the sixty-five pages. I really thought they were excellent. And so amusingly written. You have done a fine job . . . Love, Hitch.'

Buoyed by his words and galvanized into action, I spent the next several months attacking my reluctant Underwood typewriter in fits and starts, while at the other end of the building, Hitch and his staff moved in and began preparing, sketching, casting and designing the picture we called, at one time or another, 'In a Northwesterly Direction', 'The Man in Lincoln's Nose,' and 'North by Northwest', working titles, of course, telling ourselves we'd come up with the *real* title one day (and neither Hitch nor I realized until after the movie's release that, technically, there was no such direction as NNW).

Finally, disaster struck. My Underwood had fallen silent. For two whole weeks, I couldn't think of a word to write. Cary Grant had started on salary. Hitch was busy wardrobing Eva Marie Saint, and there I was with no third act, just blank pages. I had no idea why *anybody* was headed for the vicinity of Mount Rushmore.

I picked up the phone. 'Hitch, we're in trouble.'

'I'll be right there,' he said quickly. He didn't want trouble in *his* office. I gave him the bad news. We sat staring at each other.

'We'll hire a mystery writer,' he said. 'A novelist, to come in and throw ideas at us.'

'But what'll they say upstairs?' I cried. 'I'm supposed to be the writer!'

'I'll tell them it's my fault,' he said. 'I wasn't able to help you enough.' I kept looking at Hitch and I really was listening to him as he slowly listed the names of all the famous suspense novelists of the day. But suddenly my right brain spoke up, and I heard myself saying, 'She takes a gun out of her purse and shoots him.'

Hitch's eyes widened. 'In the Polish Underground, sometimes they killed one of their own to show that *they* weren't one of them.'

'Hitch,' I said, 'they're not real. They're fake bullets.' After that, it was easy. The whole third act fell into place just like that.

These days, as always, movie-goers like to find holes in the story. I usually offer them a fleet of trucks. Only the other day, I drove through a new hole myself. Thornhill is peering through binoculars at the faces of the presidents. 'I don't like the way Teddy Roosevelt is looking at me,' he says uneasily to the Professor, seated nearby. Go see the picture again. The way his face is positioned. Teddy Roosevelt isn't looking at *anyone*.

Ernest Lehman, 1999

# CREDITS

# North by Northwest

## A SERIES OF STREET SCENES

*Over them, the credits. These scenes should capture the tempo of
Madison Avenue and Fifth Avenue in the fifties. Streets swarming with
smartly dressed people. Revolving doors of sleek glass-and-steel office
buildings spewing out streams of super-charged New Yorkers, hurrying
for cabs and buses and subways and cocktail bars. Two bundle-laden
women fighting over a cab. A packed bus closing its doors in the face of
an irate would-be passenger. A newsboy in front of the Independent
Subway entrance. 'Trouble in the Middle East! Evening papers! Get
your trouble in the Middle East!'*

## INT. LOBBY OF OFFICE BUILDING — MADISON AVENUE

*Four elevators in action. A starter keeping things humming. Doors close
on an elevator. It starts up. Another elevator arrives at street level. The
last credit fades. The elevator doors open. Crowds pour out, and we hear
a voice at the rear of the car even before the man is revealed to us by the
off-going passengers. He is Roger Thornhill, tall, lean, faultlessly dressed
(and far too original to be wearing the gray-flannel uniform of his
kind). He has been dictating to his secretary, Maggie, an ageing,
unbeautiful woman who has accompanied him down in the elevator
with pad and pencil in hand. She will have to scurry to keep up with his
impatient stride when they leave the elevator and cross the lobby to the
entrance.*

> THORNHILL
> *(dictating)*
> . . . Even if you accept the belief that a high Trendex
> automatically means a rising sales curve, which incidentally I
> do *not* accept . . .
> *(to elevator starter)*
> 'Night, Eddie.

> STARTER
> Mr Thornhill.

**THORNHILL**

Say hello to the missus.

**STARTER**
(*sourly*)

We're not talking.

**THORNHILL**
(*to Maggie, continuing dictation as they cross lobby*)

My recommendation is still the same. Dash. Spread the good word in as many small-time segments as we can grab . . .

(*as he pauses at the news-stand, buys a paper*)

. . . And let the opposition have their high ratings, while we cry about it all the way to the bank.

(*moving on*)

Why don't we colonize at the Colony one day next week for lunch? Let me hear from you, Sam. Happy thoughts. Etcetera . . .

(*they are at the entrance now*)

Better walk me to the Plaza.

**MAGGIE**
(*a weary moan*)

Walk?

**THORNHILL**

Use your blood sugar. Come on.

*He eases her through the door, follows her to the sidewalk.*

**EXT. STREET – TRACKING SHOT**

*They start to walk west, Thornhill glancing at the newspaper as he goes.*

**THORNHILL**

Next?

**MAGGIE**
(*consulting her pad*)

Gretchen Sabinson.

**THORNHILL**
(*grimaces*)

Send her a box of candy from Blum's. Ten dollars. The kind

4

. . . you know . . . each piece wrapped in gold paper? She'll like that. She'll think she's eating money. Say: 'Darling, I count the days, the hours, the minutes –'

MAGGIE
(*interrupting*)

You sent that one last time.

THORNHILL

Did I? Then just say: 'Something for your sweet tooth, honey . . . and all your other sweet parts.'
(*Maggie gives him a look and he winces*)
I know, I know.

MAGGIE

Could we take a cab, Mr Thornhill?

THORNHILL

A couple of blocks?

MAGGIE

You're late and I'm tired.

THORNHILL

I keep telling you, Maggie, you don't eat properly.
(*steps off the curb, tries to flag a cab*)
Taxi! . . . Taxi!

*He is getting nowhere. Just then, a taxi pulls up before a man who has also been seeking one. Quickly Thornhill darts over and opens the door.*

(*to the man*)

I have a sick woman here. Would you mind terribly?

MAN
(*a little bewildered*)

Why no . . . I mean –

THORNHILL
(*quickly*)

Thank you very much.

*He quickly bundles Maggie into the cab, follows her in and slams the door shut.*

MAN
(*still befuddled*)

Perfectly all right . . .

*The cab pulls away.*

INT. CAB

THORNHILL
(*to driver*)

First stop, the Plaza. Don't throw the flag.

MAGGIE
(*looking back*)

Poor man.

THORNHILL

Poor man nothing. I made him a Good Samaritan.

MAGGIE

He knew you were lying.

THORNHILL
(*opening up the newspaper again*)

In the world of advertising there is no such thing as a lie, Maggie. There is only The Expedient Exaggeration. Do I look a little heavyish to you?

MAGGIE

What?

THORNHILL

I *feel* heavyish. Put a note on my desk in the morning. 'Think thin.'

MAGGIE
(*writing*)

Think thin.

THORNHILL
(*to the driver*)

Make it the Fifty-ninth Street entrance, driver.

DRIVER

Okay.

THORNHILL
(*to Maggie, as he continues to peruse the newspaper*)
Soon as you get back to the office, call my mother, tell her
about the theatre tickets for tonight. Dinner at Twenty-One,
seven o'clock. I'll have had two Martinis at the Oak Bar, so
she needn't bother to sniff me.

MAGGIE

She doesn't do *that*.

THORNHILL

Like a bloodhound.

*As the cab pulls up before the Fifty-ninth Street entrance to the Plaza:*

MAGGIE
(*reading from notes*)
Bigelow at ten-thirty is your first for tomorrow. You're due at
the Skin Glow rehearsal at noon. Then lunch with Falcon and
his wife –

THORNHILL
(*handing her some money*)
Oh, yes. Where was that?

MAGGIE

Larry and Arnold's. One o'clock.

*Thornhill has dropped his newspaper on the seat and is on his way out
of the cab.*

Will you check in later?

EXT. PLAZA HOTEL

THORNHILL
(*now out of the cab*)
Absolutely not.
(*to driver*)
Take this lady back where she belongs.

7

**DRIVER**

Right.

**THORNHILL**
(*to Maggie*)
Don't forget to call my mother right away.

**MAGGIE**
I won't. Goodnight, Mr Thornhill.

*Thornhill slams the door and the cab starts away. Suddenly he remembers something, snaps his fingers, points after the cab.*

**THORNHILL**
Wait a minute! You *can't* call her! She's at Mrs –

*He stops. The cab is already on its way. He stands there for a moment looking after it. Then he goes up the steps into the hotel.*

INT. LOBBY PLAZA HOTEL

*Thornhill glances at his wrist-watch as he crosses the lobby to the Oak Bar.*

INT. OAK BAR

*Thornhill pauses in the entrance, looking about impatiently. The Captain comes up to him.*

**CAPTAIN**
Evening, Mr Thornhill.

**THORNHILL**
Hello, Victor. I'm looking for Herman Weltner and two gentlemen –

**CAPTAIN**
(*pointing*)
Yes. Right over there.

**THORNHILL**
Oh yes.

*Thornhill walks to a far corner of the room to the table where Weltner, an Ivy-League costumed executive, is seated with a Mr Nelson and a*

*Mr Wade, both of whom look like out-of-town sponsors, which they are.*

> WELTNER
> (*rising to his feet*)

Roger.

> THORNHILL
> (*shaking his hand*)

Herman. Sorry I'm so late.

> WELTNER
> (*making introductions*)

This is Roger Thornhill. Fanning Nelson –

*Nelson cups a hand to his ear.*

> THORNHILL
> (*shaking his other hand*)

Delighted.

> WELTNER

And Larry Wade.

> THORNHILL
> (*shaking hands*)

How do you do, Mr Wade?

> WADE
> (*indicating his drink*)

We've gotten a little head start here, Mr Thornhill.

> THORNHILL

Won't last for long.

*He sits down, looking about nervously.*

> WELTNER

I was just telling Larry and Fanning here that you may be slow in starting but there's nobody faster down the homestretch.
> (*noting Thornhill's nervousness*)
> What's the matter, Roger? You've got the fidgets.

*During the following, a Bellboy will enter the room and move among the tables calling out: 'Paging Mr George Kaplan!' Standing in the entrance watching the Bellboy's progress (and observed by us if we happen to be looking off into background) are two rather unobtrusive-looking Men:*

#### THORNHILL
Something very silly. I told my secretary to call my mother, and I just remembered, she's not going to be able to reach her in time.

#### WELTNER
Why not?

#### THORNHILL
Because she's playing bridge at the apartment of one of her cronies . . .

#### WELTNER
Your secretary?

#### THORNHILL
No. My mother. And it's one of those brand-new apartments – all wet paint and no telephone yet.

#### NELSON
(*cupping his ear*)
What was that?

*Thornhill looks at him with astonishment.*

#### BELLBOY
(*approaching*)
Paging Mr George Kaplan!

#### THORNHILL
(*musing*)
I think maybe if I send her a telegram . . .

#### BELLBOY
(*closer*)
Mr George Kaplan!

THORNHILL
(*signaling the boy*)
Boy – would you come here please?

CUT TO:

CLOSE ANGLE: THE TWO MEN STANDING IN ENTRANCE TO ROOM
*They react with sudden interest, glance at each other, then look off
again and see:*

POINT OF VIEW: FROM ENTRANCE
*The Bellboy moving up to Thornhill, whose table is well out of earshot of
the entrance.*

CLOSE ANGLE: THE TABLE
*Thornhill takes a pen and a long envelope from his inside pocket as he
addresses the Bellboy:*

THORNHILL
Look, I've got to get a wire off immediately. Can you send it
for me if I write it out for you?

BELLBOY
I'm not permitted to do that, sir, but if you'll follow me –

THORNHILL
(*to the others at the table*)
Will you excuse me for a moment?

WADE
Go right ahead.

NELSON
(*cupping his ear*)
What was that?

*Thornhill gives him a quick look.*

THORNHILL
(*to Weltner, as he gets up*)
Herman, if you can scare up a double Martini . . .

WELTNER

Sure thing.

*Thornhill walks off with the Bellboy.*

NELSON
(*turning to Wade*)

Where's he going?

WADE

There's no telephone where his mother is playing bridge.

NELSON
(*stares at him a moment*)

Why not?

*Now Wade gives him a look.*

OUTSIDE THE OAK BAR

*Thornhill and the Bellboy emerge from the room.*

BELLBOY
(*pointing*)

Right there, sir.

THORNHILL
(*giving him a tip*)

Thanks.

BELLBOY

Thank *you*, sir.

*Thornhill starts towards the Western Union office, as the Bellboy goes off in another direction. Suddenly the two 'unobtrusive' Men walk swiftly into the shot directly behind Thornhill. One of them, who we now see has a scar on the corner of his right eye, taps him on the shoulder. He pauses and turns.*

THORNHILL

Yes?

FIRST MAN
(*with a faint foreign accent*)
The car is waiting outside. You will walk between us saying nothing.

THORNHILL
What are you talking about?

SECOND MAN
(*taking Thornhill's arm*)
Let's go.

THORNHILL
Go where? Who *are* you?

FIRST MAN
Mere errand boys, carrying concealed weapons. His is pointed at your heart, so, please, no errors of judgement, I beg of you.

THORNHILL
(*pulling free*)
What is this – a joke or something?

SECOND MAN
Yes. A joke.
(*he removes his hand from his pocket, shoves a gun into Thornhill's ribs*)
We will laugh in the car.

*Thornhill stares at the man for a moment.*

THORNHILL
This is ridiculous.

*The Man nods towards the side entrance and Thornhill starts away, flanked on either side.*

EXT. STREET

*Thornhill emerges from the hotel to the sidewalk. The Men take his arms and ease him inconspicuously past unnoticing passersby to a limousine parked at the curb. They open the rear door, push Thornhill into the back seat and follow him in. A third Man sitting behind the wheel immediately starts the car and pulls away.*

13

INT. CAR

*As the car moves east, Thornhill glances at the stony-faced men on either side of him. He is anxious, but does not want to show it.*

THORNHILL
Don't tell me where we're going. Surprise me.

*The Men stare straight ahead, saying nothing.*

Y'know, I left some people waiting for me back there in the Oak Bar, and they're going to think I'm awfully rude, going off like this.
(*he waits – no response*)
I mean, if you could let me off at a drugstore for a moment, I could call and explain that I'm . . .
(*he glances at the men inquiringly*)
. . . being . . . kidnapped?
(*no response*)
That *is* what's happening, isn't it?

*No answer. His glance goes to the door handle. The car has stopped for a red light. Suddenly he lunges for the door and struggles to open it, as the two Men watch him calmly. Apparently the door has special locks. It will not budge. Thornhill takes his seat again and points sheepishly to the door.*

Locked.

DISSOLVE TO:

EXT. GLEN COVE ESTATE – DUSK

*The car approaches the entrance to a magnificent estate. On the open gate, a nameplate:* TOWNSEND. *The car turns into the driveway.*

INT. CAR

*Thornhill, flanked by the two Men, is looking over his shoulder at the receding gates. He turns forward, looks at one of the Men.*

THORNHILL
Who's Townsend?

14

*No answer. He glances at the other man questioningly. More stony silence.*

Oh, really? Interesting.

*Then he looks out ahead.*

**MOVING POINT OF VIEW**

*A curving, tree-lined driveway. Through the trees, a red-brick mansion.*

**INT. CAR**

*Thornhill is still looking out.*

**EXT. MAIN HOUSE**

*An impressive though considerably faded mansion of the early twenties. The car swings around the circular driveway, pulls up before the entrance. Thornhill and the two Men get out. One of the Men (he of the scarred eye – his name is Valerian) accompanies Thornhill up the steps to the front door. The other man (Licht) follows them and waits until the door opens before he moves away and follows a path to the rear of the house. After a moment, a stocky, gray-haired woman wearing the uniform of a Housekeeper opens the front door. Valerian walks Thornhill right in past her.*

**INT. HOUSE**

*Beyond the oval foyer, a curving marble staircase leads to a balcony, off which are many rooms. Above the balcony, a stained-glass window. Everywhere, a kind of seedy grandeur.*

**VALERIAN**
(*to housekeeper*)

Where is he?

**HOUSEKEEPER**

Upstairs, dressing.

**VALERIAN**

Tell him I'm here.

15

HOUSEKEEPER

The dinner guests are expected.

VALERIAN
(*impatiently*)

Never mind. Say to him 'Kaplan'.

*At this, the woman glances at Thornhill.*

THORNHILL

By the way – what are we having for dessert?

VALERIAN
(*to Housekeeper*)

Is anyone in the library?

HOUSEKEEPER

No.

VALERIAN
(*to Thornhill, brusquely*)

This way.

*He walks Thornhill to the library door, as the Housekeeper goes upstairs.*

INT. LIBRARY

*Books, from floor to ceiling. And windows overlooking the rear lawn. In the distance, Long Island Sound. Valerian opens the door, gestures to Thornhill, who enters.*

VALERIAN
(*his hand on the key*)

You will wait here.

THORNHILL
(*indicating the shelves of books*)

Don't hurry. I'll catch up on my reading.

*Valerian closes the door behind him. Immediately, Thornhill goes to the door to open it. Just as his hand reaches the knob, he hears the door being locked from the outside. He tries it anyway, then turns, glances around, walks to the desk, sees several magazines there:* Field and Stream . . . Newsweek . . . Fortune . . . *etc. In an* INSERT, *he and*

we see that the addressee on all of them is: 'Mr Lester Townsend,
Baywood, Glen Cove, NY'. *Thornhill steps to a window, peers out.*

### EXT. BACK LAWN

THORNHILL'S POINT OF VIEW: *a man is playing croquet all by
himself in the fading light. His name is Leonard. Later, we will see him
at closer range. He is about thirty, but looks much younger, for he has a
soft baby-face, large eyes and hair that falls down over his forehead. His
attitudes are unmistakably effeminate. Hurrying towards him is Licht,
the other abductor. In a brief pantomime, Licht apparently gives
Leonard tidings, and they quickly go off together towards the house.*

### INT. LIBRARY

*Seeing the back lawn now deserted, Thornhill tries to open the window
to escape. It is locked. He unfastens the catch, raises the window, is
about to climb out when he draws back and turns at the sound of the
door opening behind him. In walks a distinguished looking Man of
about forty, professorial in manner but definitely sexually attractive (to
women), and only slightly sinister.*

> MAN
> (*affably*)

Good evening . . .

*He holds out his hand. Thornhill takes it uncertainly.*

> THORNHILL

Not a moment too soon.

> MAN
> (*scrutinizing him*)

Well – so . . .

> THORNHILL

Thank you. That explains everything.

> MAN
> (*still peering at him*)

. . . Not what I expected – a little taller, a little more polished
than the others . . .

THORNHILL
(*with bite*)
I'm so glad you're pleased, Mr Townsend.

MAN
(*reacts, then smiles*)
. . . But I'm afraid just as obvious.

THORNHILL
Forgive me for being obvious, but what the devil is this all about? Why was I brought here?

MAN
(*wearily*)
Games? . . . Must we?

THORNHILL
Not that I mind a slight case of abduction now and then, but I do have tickets to the theatre tonight and it was a show I was looking forward to and I get, well, kind of *unreasonable* about things like that.

MAN
With such expert play-acting, you make this very room a theatre.
(*the man of the croquet wickets enters*)
Ah – Leonard. Have you met our distinguished guest?

LEONARD
(*staring at Thornhill*)
He's a well-tailored one, isn't he?

*Thornhill gives him a look of distaste.*

MAN
My secretary is a great admirer of your methods, Mr Kaplan. Elusiveness, however misguided –

THORNHILL
(*interrupting*)
Wait a minute. Did you call me Kaplan?

MAN
Oh, I know you're a man of many names, but I'm perfectly willing to accept your current choice.

**THORNHILL**

Current choice? My name is Thornhill – Roger Thornhill – and it's never been anything else.

**MAN**

Of course . . .

*Leonard starts to chuckle.*

**THORNHILL**
*(smiling)*

Obviously your friends picked up the wrong package when they bundled me out here in the car.

**MAN**
*(tired of all this)*

Sit down, Mr Kaplan, won't you?

**THORNHILL**
*(the smile fades)*

I told you: I'm not Kaplan, whoever *he* is. I'm Roger Thornhill of the Wadley and Rapp Agency, and unless you gentlemen happen to be interested in *advertising* something, this meeting is going to turn out to be an enormous bust for all concerned.

*There is a knock on the door. It opens and a handsome Woman in her forties peers in.*

**WOMAN**

Excuse me –

**MAN**
*(politely)*

Yes?

**WOMAN**

The guests are here.

**MAN**

Look after them. I'll be with you in a few minutes.

THORNHILL
(*turning on her with sarcasm*)
Don't bother to set a place for me, Mrs Townsend. I won't be staying for dinner.

*She gives a flustered glance in the direction of the men, then hurriedly withdraws, and closes the door.*

MAN
(*to Thornhill*)
Now – shall we get down to business?

THORNHILL
I'm all for that.

MAN
Quite simply, I'd like you to tell me how much you know of our arrangements and – of course – how you've *come* by this information. Naturally, I don't expect to get this for nothing.

THORNHILL
(*with a sarcastic bow of the head*)
Of course not.

MAN
Don't misunderstand me. I don't really expect you to fall in with my suggestion, but the least I can do is afford you the opportunity of surviving the evening –

THORNHILL
(*frowns*)
Surviving the evening . . .?

MAN
Now why don't you surprise me, Mr Kaplan, and say 'yes'?

THORNHILL
I already told you –

LEONARD
(*interrupting*)
We know where you're headed for . . .

THORNHILL
(*turning on him*)

I'm headed for the Winter Garden Theatre in New York, and
I think I better get going.

*He goes to the door, flings it open, sees Valerian standing there blocking
the entrance. He turns.*

Townsend – you're making a serious mistake . . .

*Leonard eases over and closes the door again as the Man, walking to
the desk, says:*

MAN

This is not going to lead to a very happy conclusion, Mr
Kaplan –

THORNHILL

I'm not Kaplan!

MAN

I do wish you would reconsider.

LEONARD

We also know your contact in Pittsburgh since Jason
committed suicide.

THORNHILL
(*angrily*)

What contact? I've never even *been* in Pittsburgh.

*The other Man is at the desk, looking down at a piece of paper as he
speaks quickly:*

MAN

On June sixteenth, you checked into the Sherwyn Hotel in
Pittsburgh as Mr George Kaplan of Berkeley, California. A
week later you registered at the Benjamin Franklin Hotel in
Philadelphia as Mr George Kaplan of Pittsburgh. On August
eleventh you stayed at the Statler in Boston. On August
twenty-ninth George Kaplan of Boston registered at the
Whittier in Detroit. At present, you are registered in room
seven ninety-six at the Plaza Hotel in New York as Mr
George Kaplan of Detroit –

THORNHILL

(*tersely*)

What else?

MAN

– In two days, you are due at the Ambassador East in
Chicago –

THORNHILL

Oh?

MAN

– And then at the Sheraton-Johnson Hotel in Rapid City,
South Dakota.

THORNHILL

(*shaking his head*)

Not me.

MAN

– So you see, there is little sense in maintaining this fiction
that you are deceiving us, any more than *we* are deceiving *you*,
Mr Kaplan.

*Thornhill stares at him for a long moment, helplessly frustrated.*

THORNHILL

I don't suppose it would do any good to show you a wallet
full of identification cards, a driver's license, things like that?

LEONARD

(*shakes his head*)

They provide you with such *good* ones.

MAN

(*quietly*)

It's getting late. Do you intend to cooperate with us? I'd like a
simple yes or no.

THORNHILL

(*completely exasperated*)

All right. A simple no. For the simple reason that I simply
don't know what you're talking about.

MAN
(*turns to his secretary*)
Give Mr Kaplan a drink, Leonard.
(*he turns to Thornhill*)
A pleasant journey, sir.

*The Man goes to the door, opens it, holds it open for a fraction.*
*Valerian and Licht enter. The Man leaves, closing the door behind him.*
*Leonard opens a cabinet. Liquor bottles are seen. He turns to Thornhill.*

LEONARD
Scotch? Rye? Bourbon? Vodka?

THORNHILL
Nothing. I'll just take a quick ride back to town.

LEONARD
That has been arranged . . .

*Thornhill glances at the deadpan faces of Valerian and Licht with*
*growing apprehension.*

But first, a libation.

*Leonard reaches into the cabinet, takes out a large bottle of whiskey. He*
*holds it up.*

Bourbon.

*He moves towards Thornhill with the bottle.*

THORNHILL
You have some. I've had enough stimulation for one day.

LEONARD
(*gently*)
It will be easier if you take this yourself. Otherwise, it will be
necessary for us to insist.

*Thornhill's eyes widen. He points at the bottle.*

THORNHILL
The whole quart?

LEONARD
Not a quart, Mr Kaplan. It's only a fifth.

23

*Thornhill makes a sudden move, tries to go past him to the door, but Valerian and Licht grab him, pin his arms behind him. As they do so, camera dollies in to a full head and shoulders shot of Thornhill, who stares off screen. We hear the pop of the cork being drawn from the bottle. Then Leonard's hand comes up into the shot holding an empty tumbler.*

**LEONARD'S VOICE**
*(off-screen)*

Cheers.

*Now the bottle comes into shot and begins to fill the tumbler with bourbon before Thornhill's staring face.*

DISSOLVE TO:

EXT. HILL ROAD — NIGHT

*Two cars are making their way along a winding, precipitous road. The leading car is a light-colored open Mercedes Benz. Behind it is the limousine which brought Thornhill from the Plaza Hotel to Glen Cove. We hear Thornhill's voice coming from the leading car in drunken song:*

'*Somewhere I'll find you . . . Sneak up behind you . . .*' *The two cars come to a stop at the top of the hill. The driver of the limousine gets out quickly and we see that it is Licht. He crosses over swiftly to the Mercedes Benz.*

CLOSE ANGLE: THE MERCEDES BENZ
*The driver of the Mercedes Benz – Valerian – is just getting out as Licht arrives. Sitting in the Mercedes Benz, mumbling and singing drunkenly, is Thornhill.*

> THORNHILL
> (*with gestures*)
> G'night Mr Townsend . . . Mizz Townsend . . . 'night . . .
> Parting such sweet sorrow . . .
> > (*sings*)
> '*I've grown accustomed to your . . . bourbon . . .*'

*During this, the two Men have held a brief, sharp exchange in a foreign tongue. Valerian takes a quick step towards the edge and sees:*

POINT OF VIEW
*The winding, descending, precipitous road ahead.*

CLOSE ANGLE: THE MERCEDES BENZ
*Valerian turns back and with the help of Licht hurriedly pulls Thornhill into the driver's seat. Then, as Licht runs to the limousine, Valerian gets into the Mercedes Benz beside Thornhill, reaches across and starts the motor.*

> THORNHILL
> (*mumbles*)
> Don't worry about me, fellahs. I'll take the bus from here.

INT. MERCEDES BENZ

*Valerian releases the handbrake, pushes Thornhill back, takes the wheel and applies his left foot to the accelerator. As the car starts to move, Valerian glances ahead tensely.*

POINT OF VIEW
*The car is approaching a precipice.*

**INT. MERCEDES BENZ**

*Valerian opens the door at his side and gets ready to jump. Just then, Thornhill, opening a bleary eye, begins to sense what is happening. He turns, puts both hands on Valerian and gives him a violent shove, saying thickly:*

> **THORNHILL**
> You take the bus too.

*Valerian falls out of the car. Thornhill grabs the wheel and turns it sharply.*

**EXT. MERCEDES BENZ**

*The outside wheels travel along the edge of the precipice.*

**THORNHILL AT THE WHEEL**
*Looks ahead, only slightly aware of his danger. He gives the wheel another wrench.*

**CLOSE-UP: MERCEDES BENZ**
*The rear outside wheel is over the edge, spins in mid-air for a moment. Then the inner wheel gets a grip on the crumbling edge, and the car shoots forward.*

**CLOSE-UP: THORNHILL AT THE WHEEL**
*He turns, glances back, sees:*

**POINT OF VIEW:**
*Valerian in the act of getting into the already moving limousine.*

**EXT. MERCEDES BENZ**

*It picks up speed and goes careening down the winding, precipitous road.*

**EXT. LIMOUSINE**

*Valerian and Licht are in hot and angry pursuit.*

## THE CHASE SEQUENCE

*The Mercedes Benz can take the sharp curves with more ease than the limousine. Also, Thornhill is too far gone to know that he shouldn't drive that fast. Consequently, he gets to the foot of the hill and down to a main thoroughfare still in the lead. Naturally, we film this ride, and that which follows, from many different angles, including Thornhill's delirious double-vision point of view. He will be killed if he is caught, and he will be killed if he keeps driving this way. There is very little choice really. On the highway now, he is doing eighty, weaving wildly through traffic, swerving suicidally over double lanes and giving heart failure to oncoming truck drivers. But he is leaving the limousine behind.*

## A POLICE CAR

*Two Officers in the front seat. The car is travelling along at a normal speed. Suddenly Thornhill's car comes dashing by. The officers react immediately, start in pursuit.*

## INT. LIMOUSINE

*Valerian and Licht see the police car, which is almost directly in front of them, take off after Thornhill. Valerian signals to Licht to slow down. Licht does so, and starts to make a U-turn.*

## INT. THE MERCEDES BENZ

*Thornhill tries desperately to keep his eyes in focus, his foot on the floorboard and his hands on the wheel. Horns blare warningly as he comes perilously close to several head-on crashes. In his rear-view mirror, he sees the headlights of the police car following and does not realize that it is no longer the limousine. The headlights are coming closer. Suddenly, almost too late, he sees ahead of him an elderly gentleman on a bicycle emerge from a side road. He slams on the brakes and the car comes to a screaming, wobbling stop. The bicyclist, oblivious, continues across.*

## SIDE ANGLE
*As Thornhill's car comes to a final, jerking halt, the police car, with screaming brakes, hits Thornhill's rear. There is a crunching sound as*

27

*the bonnet of the police car crumples like tin. There is a momentary
silence and then the sudden scream of more brakes, and a third car
smashes into the back of the police car, giving it a crumpled rear as well.
Thornhill drunkenly leans out and looks behind to see what all the fuss
is about. The two Police Officers, after forcing a door open, emerge,
glowering. At the same time, the third driver is seen getting out of his
car, somewhat bewildered, and starting forward.*

DISSOLVE TO:

INT. GLEN COVE POLICE STATION – NIGHT

*A Lieutenant Hagerman is behind the desk. To his right is a radiophone
transmitter-receiver, over which we hear the faint communications of
cruising police cars and their patrol stations. A commotion is heard
outside, and then one of the police-car Officers, a gentleman known as
Sergeant Klinger, escorts a wobbly Thornhill into the building.*

THORNHILL
(*thickly*)
Thanks for the lift, fellahs.

KLINGER
Lieutenant – I want this man examined for driving while
intoxicated.

LIEUTENANT
(*looking at the swaying Thornhill*)
Really?

THORNHILL
(*to the lieutenant*)
They tried to kill me . . . He won't listen . . . Big house . . .
They tried to kill me.

KLINGER
(*during above*)
All right. Let's just go inside . . .

THORNHILL
(*moving with him*)
Don't wanna go inside. Somebody call the police.

28

*The Sergeant leads Thornhill by the arm into the courtroom.*

INT. COURTROOM

*A bleak room at this late hour of night.*

> KLINGER
> *(indicating a chair)*

Sit down.

> THORNHILL

Don't wanna sit. Perfectly all right.
> *(he falls into the seat)*

We'll throw the book at 'em. Kidnapping. Assault with gun
. . . and bourbon . . . and sports car. *We'll* get 'em.

> KLINGER

You'll be all right after a good night's sleep. We got a nice cell
all made up and waiting.

> THORNHILL

Don't wanna cell. I want a policeman.

*The other arresting officer, Patrolman Waggoner, enters.*

> WAGGONER

The car was just reported stolen.

> KLINGER

Uh huh.

> WAGGONER

A Mrs Babson up on Twining Road.

> THORNHILL
> *(getting unsteadily to his feet)*

Gotta call someone. Where's the phone?

> KLINGER

You're allowed one call. Right over here.
> *(leads Thornhill to a nearby phone)*

Better make it your lawyer.

THORNHILL
(*to Klinger*)
Butterfield eight-one-oh-nine-eight.

KLINGER
What am I – a telephone operator?

THORNHILL
(*nodding*)
Yeah. Butterfield eight-one-oh-nine-eight.

*Reluctantly, Klinger puts the call through. After a few moments:*

KLINGER
(*to phone*)
Just a minute please . . . Here.

*He hands the phone to Thornhill.*

THORNHILL
(*to phone*)
Hello, Mother? This is your son, Roger Thornhill.
(*listens*)
Wait a minute.
(*to Klinger*)
Where am I?

KLINGER
Glen Cove Police Station.

THORNHILL
(*to phone*)
Glen Cove Police Station . . .
(*listens*)
Now is that a nice thing to say, Mother? I have *not* been
drinking again. But these two fellows poured a bottle of
bourbon down my throat –
(*listens, shakes his head*)
No. They didn't give me a chaser . . .

*During above, Dr Cross, a pleasant young physician, has entered.
Klinger comes over, interrupts Thornhill.*

Wait a minute, Mother.

(to Klinger)

Not finished yet.

**KLINGER**

Yes you are. C'mon.

**THORNHILL**
(to phone)

Gotta hang up now, Mother. You better get my lawyer right away and bail me out.

**KLINGER**

Tomorrow morning, tell her.

**THORNHILL**
(to phone)

He says 'tomorrow morning'.
(listens)

I don't know. I'll ask him.
(to Klinger)

She wants to know *who* says.

**KLINGER**

Sergeant Emil Klinger

**THORNHILL**
(to phone)

Sergeant Emil –
(a double take at the Sergeant)
*Emil?*
(to phone)

Sergeant Emil Klinger.
(listens)

No. I didn't believe it either.
(listens)

Don't worry. I'm all right, Mother. 'Nightie night.
(he hangs up)

That was Mother.

*Klinger leads him over to a table where Dr Cross is waiting with medical kit.*

31

*(to Dr Cross)*

Here's your man, Doctor.

*Cross glances at Thornhill, indicates a chair. Thornhill collapses into it. Klinger and Patrolman Waggoner move into background as silent observers. Cross takes out a questionnaire and a fountain pen, begins to fill out the form, quickly and perfunctorily.*

DR CROSS

What's your name?

THORNHILL

Roger Thornhill. Don't believe we've met.

DR CROSS

Address?

THORNHILL

Eighty-four Sutton Place. Doctor, you listen to me –

DR CROSS

Were you operating the motor vehicle in question?

THORNHILL

Admirably.

DR CROSS

Where were you going?

THORNHILL

No place. Just trying to get away from some fellahs who were trying to kill me. I've been trying to tell these –

DR CROSS

Where did you start from?

THORNHILL

Big house. I don't know where. Big house. And these fellahs –

DR CROSS
*(interrupting)*

Stand up please, Mr Thornhill . . .

THORNHILL
(*struggling to his feet*)

Sure.

DR CROSS
(*throwing some coins on the floor*)

. . . And pick up those coins.

THORNHILL
(*looking right at the money*)

What coins?

DR CROSS
(*pointing to a white line on the floor*)

Never mind. Now I want you to walk that line.

THORNHILL
(*as he tries unsuccessfully to negotiate the line*)

At first I thought they were gonna hold me for ransom. They
brought me to this house. Can't remember the guy's name
right now. Think it was Kaplan. Yeah, George Kaplan –

*He stops abruptly as he falls to the floor. Then, as he starts to get to his
feet again:*

DR CROSS

Ever have diabetes?

THORNHILL

Never touch the stuff.

DR CROSS

Then you're not taking insulin.

THORNHILL

Never touch the stuff.

DR CROSS

Have you used a mouthwash recently?

THORNHILL

Never stuch the tuff.

DR CROSS

Stick out your tongue and say 'ah'.

33

**THORNHILL**

Better move back . . . Ah-h-h!

**DR CROSS**

Have you been drinking?

**THORNHILL**

Doctor – I am gassed.

**DR CROSS**

What were you drinking?

**THORNHILL**

Bourbon. They held me down and another guy –

**DR CROSS**

How much would you say you drank?

**THORNHILL**
(*holding his palms about a foot apart*)

About this much.

*He starts towards a long table as:*

**DR CROSS**

Mr Thornhill – it is my opinion that you are definitely
intoxicated . . .
(*as Thornhill lies down on the table*)
. . . And I am now going to have to ask your permission to
draw blood.

**THORNHILL**
(*a sleepy murmur*)

How disgusting.

**DR CROSS**
(*reading very quickly from his questionnaire*)

'You may refuse to permit a blood test to be made, but if you
do refuse, your license will be revoked. You have the right to
notify a physician of your own choosing to administer this
chemical test if you so prefer.'
(*looking up*)
Is that understood, Mr Thornhill?
(*no response*)

34

Mr Thornhill?

*Sergeant Klinger steps forward, puts a finger to his lips.*

### KLINGER

Shhh . . .

*He looks down at Thornhill with mock tenderness. Now we see Thornhill. He is sleeping like a baby, with a little smile on his face.*

DISSOLVE TO:

INT. COURTROOM — NEXT MORNING

*The judge, Anson B. Flynn, is staring coldly down at Thornhill, who, looking plenty the worse for a night in jail, stands between his attorney, Victor Larrabee, and Sergeant Klinger. Seated behind them is Thornhill's mother, Clara Thornhill, a woman who has played so much bridge she is getting to look like the Queen of Hearts. During the following, Thornhill turns, smiles at her feebly. She does not smile back:*

### LARRABEE
(*speaking with ill-concealed distaste*)
– It was at this point that Mr Thornhill succeeded in *escaping* from his would-be assassins, and when they gave chase, he, naturally, had to drive as best he could under the, uh, circumstances. But unfortunately the, uh, circumstances were a little more than he could handle, and so, well, here we are.

### THORNHILL
(*half aloud*)
But where are *they*?

*The judge gives Thornhill a hard-eyed look, then turns to Larrabee.*

### JUDGE
Counsellor, how long have you known your client?

### LARRABEE
Seven years, Your Honor.

### JUDGE
Do you know him to be a reasonable man?

**LARRABEE**

Absolutely.

*In background, Mrs Thornhill gives an audible sniff of scorn. Thornhill quickly turns and gives her an angry whisper.*

**THORNHILL**

Mother!

**JUDGE**

And do you believe there is some credence to this . . . story?

**THORNHILL**
*(bridling)*

Credence!

**LARRABEE**

Well . . . yes, Your Honor. I mean if my client says that this is what happened, I am certain it must have . . .
*(he shrugs)*
. . . happened.

**JUDGE**

Mm hmm.
*(he turns to Klinger)*
Sergeant – I want this turned over to the County Detectives for investigation. I suggest you call them up and have them come over here immediately.

**KLINGER**
*(starting away)*

Right, Your Honor.

**JUDGE**

Counsellor, I'm going to set this over for final disposition tomorrow night at seven-thirty, at which time I expect you and the defendant to be here and ready to go to trial. In the meantime, the County Detectives will determine whether his story has any basis in fact –

**THORNHILL**
*(indignantly)*

*Basis in fact?* I suppose if I were brought in here *dead*, you *still* wouldn't believe – !

LARRABEE
(*interrupting*)
Now, Roger, wait a minute!

THORNHILL
I mean, after all, Your Honor, would I make *up* such a story?

JUDGE
That is precisely what we intend to find out, Mr Thornhill.

DISSOLVE TO:

EXT. GLEN COVE ROAD – DAY

*The County Detectives' Car, a plain black sedan, is cruising in the tree-lined 'estate' area of Glen Cove.*

INT. CAR

*Two detectives are up front – Lieutenant Harding and Captain Junket. In the back seat, Thornhill is quietly arguing with his mother while Victor Larrabee listens in strained silence.*

THORNHILL
. . . Because any drinking I do to excess, Mother dear, can be attributed only to the bad example set by my immediate ancestors. You are not exactly, may I remind you, addicted to *homogenized milk.*

MRS THORNHILL
Sometimes I wonder why I stand for your impertinences.

THORNHILL
You wouldn't have to if you could learn to cheat at bridge.
(*an aside to Larrabee*)
I support *all* her girl friends.

LARRABEE
Now, now, Roger . . .

MRS THORNHILL
(*scoffing*)
Not *Roger*. You forget. It's *George*.

37

(she chuckles)

George Kaplan.

**CAPTAIN JUNKET**
*(turning)*

Here's the Townsend estate. Look familiar?

**THORNHILL**
*(looking out)*

Yeah. That's it.

**EXT. THE CAR — TRAVELLING SHOT**

*The car enters the estate through the open gates, proceeds along the curving driveway and finally comes to a stop before the entrance to the main house.*

**EXT. MAIN HOUSE**

*Everyone in the car gets out. The detectives lead the way to the front door and ring the bell. Presently the door is opened by the Housekeeper, who seems not at all perturbed to see the group standing before her.*

**HOUSEKEEPER**
*(pleasantly)*

Yes?

**THORNHILL**

Remember me?

**HOUSEKEEPER**

Yes, sir.

**THORNHILL**
*(satisfied, but grim)*

Good.

**CAPTAIN JUNKET**

Is Mr Townsend at home?

**HOUSEKEEPER**

No, I'm sorry, sir. He's left for the day.

CAPTAIN JUNKET

Mrs Townsend?

HOUSEKEEPER
(*after a pause*)

Who shall I tell her is calling?

CAPTAIN JUNKET

County detectives.

HOUSEKEEPER
(*unperturbed*)

Come in, please.

*She opens the door wider.*

INT. HOUSE

*They all enter.*

HOUSEKEEPER

This way, please.

*She leads them to the library, opens the door for them and they enter.*

INT. LIBRARY

THORNHILL

This is the room.

HOUSEKEEPER

I'll call madam.

CAPTAIN JUNKET

You do that.

*The Housekeeper withdraws. Thornhill points to the settee.*

THORNHILL

There's the sofa.
(*going to the sofa*)

They spilled bourbon all over it. I'll show you the stains.

*He examines the seat cushion, frowns, turns the cushion over, frowns
even more deeply. He looks up. Everyone is staring at him. He turns,
looks about, spies the liquor cabinet.*

There's where they kept the liquor! Scotch and gin and vodka – !

MRS THORNHILL

And bourbon.

*Thornhill goes over, whips open the cabinet. It is filled with books. No liquor. Just books.*

I remember when it used to come in bottles.

*Just then the handsome Woman of the night before enters, beaming graciously and talking very fast as she goes to Thornhill.*

WOMAN

Roger! Dear!
(*he straightens up, astounded*)
We were so worried about you! Did you get home all right?
(*she embraces him*)
Of course you did. Let me look at you. A little pink-eyed and fuzzy around the cheeks. But then, aren't we all? It was a dull party really, and you didn't miss a *thing*. But Lester was furious with himself for not seeing you home personally.
(*to Clara Thornhill*)
Let's see. You must be Roger's mother. I'm so delighted to meet you. Roger's told us so much about you.
(*to Larrabee*)
And you must be a policeman. You *look* like a policeman.

LARRABEE

I am Mr Thornhill's attorney.

THORNHILL

I want everybody here to know that I never even *saw* this woman before last night!

*The Woman laughs good-naturedly at 'Roger's charming joke'. The detectives step forward.*

CAPTAIN JUNKET

Mrs Townsend – I'm Captain Junket of the Nassau County Detectives, and this is Lieutenant Harding.

#### WOMAN

How do you do?

#### LT. HARDING

Ma'am.

#### WOMAN
(*to Thornhill*)

Oh, dear. You haven't gotten into trouble, Roger . . .?

| MRS THORNHILL | THORNHILL |
|---|---|
| (*simultaneously*) | (*simultaneously*) |
| Has *he* gotten into *trouble*. | Stop calling me 'Roger'. |

#### CAPTAIN JUNKET

Mrs Townsend – Mr Thornhill was picked up last night
driving while under the influence of alcohol, and incidentally,
in a stolen car –

#### WOMAN

Stolen car?

#### CAPTAIN JUNKET

– belonging to a Mrs Babson of Twining Road –

#### WOMAN

Roger, you said you were going to call a cab. You *didn't*
borrow Laura's Mercedes?

#### THORNHILL
(*hopelessly*)

No, I *didn't* . . . *borrow* . . . *Laura's* . . . *Mercedes*.

#### CAPTAIN JUNKET

Mr Thornhill has told us that he was brought to this house
against his will last night and forcibly intoxicated by some
friends of your husband and then set out on the road. Did
you know anything about this?

*The Woman gives Thornhill a look of deep sympathy, then faces the
detectives.*

#### WOMAN

Well, now, Captain – Roger *was* a bit tipsy when he arrived
here by cab for dinner –

THORNHILL

She's lying!

WOMAN

– And I'm afraid he became even worse as the evening wore on, and finally he told us he had to go home to sleep it off. I *knew* I should have served dinner earlier. Otherwise I can assure you the harmless little escapade with Mrs Babson's car would never have happened.

THORNHILL
(*with sardonic admiration*)

What a performance!

WOMAN

Poor dear . . .

CAPTAIN JUNKET

Mrs Townsend – does the name George Kaplan mean anything to you?

WOMAN
(*blankly*)

George Kaplan? No.

CAPTAIN JUNKET

I didn't think so.

*The detective already has his eye on the door and a quick departure.*

THORNHILL
(*desperate now*)

What about her husband? He's the one you should be questioning!

CAPTAIN JUNKET
(*to the Woman*)

Is there any place he can be reached?

WOMAN

Why yes – the United Nations.

CAPTAIN JUNKET
                    (*impressed*)
The . . . United . . . Nations . . .?

WOMAN
He's addressing the General Assembly this afternoon.

*The detective looks at Thornhill and his mouth tightens.*

THORNHILL
                    (*at bay*)
All right – so he's addressing the General Assembly.

CAPTAIN JUNKET
                    (*to the Woman*)
Sorry we had to bother you.

WOMAN
No bother at all.

*She leads the group towards the door.*

THORNHILL
Wait a minute now . . .

*They go out to the foyer.*

INT. THE FOYER

*As Thornhill is hurried by his mother out of the library across the foyer, he hears:*

WOMAN'S VOICE
Will you be wanting to get in touch with my husband, Captain?

CAPTAIN JUNKET
No, Mrs Townsend – that won't be necessary.

THORNHILL
D'you mean to say you're not going to do anything more about this?

MRS THORNHILL
*(turns, fixes him with a look)*

Roger . . .

*(she shakes her head slowly)*

Pay the two dollars.

*Thornhill gives her a look, then goes out the front door with her and the others.*

EXT. MAIN HOUSE

*As the group goes down the steps and into the car, the Woman stands at the door watching. She even waves once to Thornhill, who is in no mood to wave back. On the lawn near the entrance, a gardener in overalls is on his knees working over a flower bed. His back is to the entrance, and he does not turn to see the group leave the house. But now, as the car drives off, he gets to his feet, looks after the car, then turns into camera. Beneath the overalls and the dirty face, we see Valerian.*

DISSOLVE TO:

EXT. PLAZA HOTEL. NEW YORK CITY – A FEW HOURS LATER

*A cab pulls up before the hotel. Thornhill and his mother get out and cross the sidewalk to the entrance as:*

MRS THORNHILL
I don't see what you need *me* along for.

THORNHILL
*(savagely)*
You lend me a certain air of respectability.

MRS THORNHILL
Don't be sarcastic, Roger.

*They enter the hotel.*

INT. LOBBY

*Thornhill goes to the row of house phones, saying:*

#### THORNHILL

Well, here goes.

> (*he picks up a phone*)

Do you have a George Kaplan staying here?

> (*a pause – then excitedly*)

That's right. Room seven ninety-six. Would you ring him
please?

> (*to his mother*)

It's true. He *is* registered here . . .

#### MRS THORNHILL
> (*bored*)

That's nice.

#### THORNHILL

. . . And he's just the one to clear up this little ballet.

> (*to phone*)

What? . . . Oh. I see. He didn't leave any word when he'd be
back, did he? . . . Really? All right. Thank you.

> (*he hangs up*)

That's funny. He hasn't answered his phone in two days.

#### MRS THORNHILL

Maybe he got locked in the bathroom.

*Thornhill has been peering thoughtfully towards the desk, where people
are getting their keys, mail, etc.*

#### THORNHILL

Mother – I want you to go over to the desk, put on that sweet
innocent look you do so well, and ask for the key to seven
ninety-six.

#### MRS THORNHILL

Don't be ridiculous. I wouldn't do a thing like that.

#### THORNHILL
> (*taking out a wad of bills*)

Ten dollars?

#### MRS THORNHILL

Not for all the money in the world.

Fifty?

MRS THORNHILL
(*taking the proffered money*)
You're disgraceful.

*She starts towards the desk as Thornhill watches.*

DISSOLVE TO:

INT. HOTEL CORRIDOR

*Thornhill and his mother are walking towards the door to 796.*

MRS THORNHILL
Car theft . . . drunk driving . . . assaulting an officer . . . lying
to a judge . . . and now, house-breaking . . .

THORNHILL
Not house-breaking, Mother. Hotel-breaking. There's a
difference.

MRS THORNHILL
(*gloomily*)
Of five to ten years.

*They arrive at 796; he takes the key from her hand and looks about
furtively. Then he inserts it in the lock. Just then, a chambermaid
emerges from another room, sees him and calls out:*

MAID
Just a minute please!

*Thornhill nervously pulls the key from the lock, turns and waits tensely
as she walks over to him.*

Will you be wantin' me to change your beddin', sir?

THORNHILL
(*relieved*)
Well . . . yes . . . but not right now . . .

MAID
I was only askin', sir, because the bed don't seem like it been

slept in and I was just wonderin' if I still oughta keep changin' the linens, y'know?

THORNHILL

Thank you very much for your interest.

MAID
(*smiling*)

You're welcome, sir.

*She goes off down the corridor. Quickly Thornhill inserts the key in the lock, opens the door and leads his mother into the room.*

INT. HOTEL ROOM

THORNHILL

You see that? She thought I was Kaplan. I wonder if I *look* like Kaplan.

*He glances about. There are twin beds, neatly made up, but the rest of the room looks lived-in. There is an open suitcase on the floor with a few shirts and some soiled socks in it. On a chair is a three-day stack of well-read New York newspapers. The dresser top is strewn with masculine odds and ends – an electric shaver, a pair of military brushes monogrammed 'G.K.', a half-empty pint of Canadian Club, several scribbled reminders: 'Call Wilson', 'Laundry Friday', 'Wire Ambassador East confirming reservation', 'Mahdi of Pakistan'. Also, there is a group picture torn from a newspaper. The caption is missing, but one of the faces has been ringed with red pencil. It is the face of the Man of Glen Cove.*

THORNHILL

Hmmm. Look who's here.

MRS THORNHILL
(*glancing about*)

Where? Who?

THORNHILL

Our friend who's assembling the General Assembly this afternoon.

*He puts the picture down.*

MRS THORNHILL

Roger – I think we should go.

*As he goes to the night-table and presses a button marked 'Chambermaid':*

THORNHILL

Don't be nervous, Mother.

MRS THORNHILL

I'm not nervous. I'll be late for the bridge club.

THORNHILL

Good. You'll lose less than usual.

*He goes to the bathroom and enters.*

INT. THE BATHROOM

*There are toilet articles on the sink, on the glass shelf above it, and in the medicine cabinet. Thornhill takes the comb from the hairbrush on the shelf, inspects it, then replaces it. He returns to:*

INT. THE BEDROOM

THORNHILL

Bulletin. Mr Kaplan has dandruff.

MRS THORNHILL

In that case, I think we'd better leave.

*Just then, the door buzzer sounds.*

Too late.

*Thornhill goes to the door, opens it. The Chambermaid stands there.*

MAID

You rang for me?

THORNHILL

Come in a moment.
                    (*the Maid enters*)
What's your name?

**MAID**

Elsie, sir.

**THORNHILL**

Elsie – do you know who I am?

**MAID**
(*giggles*)

Sure. You're Mr Kaplan.

**THORNHILL**

When did we . . . when did you first see me, Elsie?

**MAID**

Outside the door, out there in the hall, just a couple minutes ago. Don'tcha remember?

**THORNHILL**

You mean that's the first time you ever laid eyes on me?

**MAID**

Can I help it you're never *around*, Mr Kaplan?

**THORNHILL**

How do you know I *am* Mr Kaplan?

**MAID**
(*puzzled*)

Huh?

**THORNHILL**

How do you know I'm Mr Kaplan?

**MAID**
(*giggles*)

Well, of *course* ya are. This is room seven ninety-six, isn't it? So – you're the gentleman in room seven ninety-six, aren't ya?

**THORNHILL**

All right, Elsie.

**MAID**

Will that be all, sir?

49

THORNHILL

For the time being. Yes.

*As the Maid starts away, the door buzzer sounds again. The Maid opens the door and goes out past the Valet, who is seen standing there with a suit on a hanger.*

VALET

Valet.

THORNHILL

Come in.

VALET

*(entering)*

Hang it in the closet, Mr Kaplan?

THORNHILL

Please.

*Thornhill exchanges a look with his mother as the Valet opens the closet door, hangs the suit on the rack.*

VALET

There we are.

*(Thornhill gives him a tip)*

Thank you, Mr Kaplan.

THORNHILL

By the way – when did I give you that suit?

VALET

Last night. Around six.

THORNHILL

Did I give it to you personally?

VALET

*(smiles)*

Personally? No, Mr Kaplan. You called down on the phone and described the suit to me and said it would be hanging in the closet. Like you always do. Anything wrong?

THORNHILL

No, no. Just curious.

VALET
(leaving)

Okay. Nice meeting you, Mr Kaplan.

*He goes out. Thornhill steps to the closet, opens the door.*

### THORNHILL

I'm beginning to think nobody in this hotel has actually ever *seen* Kaplan.

### MRS THORNHILL

Maybe he has his suits mended by Invisible Weavers.

*There are several suits on the rack. Thornhill takes one out, tosses it on a chair, whips off his jacket, throws it on the bed, then takes the other jacket off the hanger and puts it on. He extends his arms. The sleeves are eight inches too short.*

(*looking him over speculatively*)
I don't think that one *does* anything for you.

*Thornhill takes the trousers from the hanger, holds them up in front of him. They are ludicrously short.*

#### THORNHILL

Look at this. They've mistaken me for a man who is only five feet tall.

#### MRS THORNHILL

I've always *told* you to stand up straight.

*Just then, the telephone on the night-table rings. Thornhill stares at it uncertainly. The phone rings again.*

#### THORNHILL

Should I?

#### MRS THORNHILL

Certainly not.

*So Thornhill goes over and picks up the receiver.*

#### THORNHILL

Hello?

#### VALERIAN'S VOICE
(*through phone*)

It is good to find you in, Mr Kaplan.

#### THORNHILL

Who is this?

#### VALERIAN'S VOICE
(*through phone*)

We met only last night and still you do not recognize my voice. I should feel offended –

#### THORNHILL

Yeah – now I know who you are and I'm *not* Mr Kaplan.

#### VALERIAN'S VOICE
(*through phone*)

Of course not. You answer his telephone and you live in his hotel room, and yet you are not Mr Kaplan. Nevertheless, we are pleased to find you in.

*He clicks off.*

#### THORNHILL

Hello?

*(jiggling receiver frantically)*

*Hello!*

#### OPERATOR'S VOICE
*(through phone)*

Yes?

#### THORNHILL

Operator, this is Mr Thorn – Mr Kaplan in seven ninety-six.
That call that just came through. Was that an *outside* call or
from the lobby?

#### OPERATOR'S VOICE
*(through phone)*

Just a minute, sir. I'll see.

#### THORNHILL

Hurry!

#### MRS THORNHILL

Who was it?

#### THORNHILL

Only one of the men who tried to kill me last night.

#### MRS THORNHILL

Oh – we're back to *that* one, are we?

#### THORNHILL
*(jiggling the phone)*

Hello – *operator!*

#### OPERATOR'S VOICE
*(through phone)*

Mr Kaplan . . .

#### THORNHILL

Yes . . .

#### OPERATOR'S VOICE
*(through phone)*

That call was made from the lobby, sir.

**THORNHILL**
It was . . .
*(he hangs up, looks about desperately)*
The lobby. They're probably on their way up right now.
Come on. We've got to get out of here.

*He struggles into his jacket, picks up the newspaper clipping and stuffs it in his pocket.*

**MRS THORNHILL**
*(not at all excited)*
I think I'd like to *meet* one of these killers.

*He takes her by the arm, hurries her to the door.*

INT. THE CORRIDOR

*As they emerge from the room, Thornhill looks about, sees no one, moves his mother swiftly to the nearby elevator. He presses the 'DOWN' button, waits anxiously. Suddenly two elevators arrive simultaneously, one from above, the other from below. Just as Thornhill and his mother enter their elevator, Valerian and Licht step out of the other one, in time to see their quarry. Before the doors can close, they quickly follow Thornhill in.*

INT. ELEVATOR

*There are six passengers in the car, all of them of obvious refinement and sophistication: an elderly gentleman and his elderly wife; two fiftyish women; and another couple. Valerian and Licht are crowded close to Thornhill and his mother as the doors close and the elevator starts down. Thornhill taps her and indicates that these are the men who are after him. She glances at them and sees two men whose attitude seems to be quite innocuous. She turns back to Thornhill and smiles her disbelief. He frowns and nods his insistence. She turns to them again and smiles.*

**MRS THORNHILL**
You gentleman aren't *really* trying to kill my son, are you?

*The men look at her blankly, as the other passengers turn their heads in surprise. Valerian starts to smile, as he turns to Licht, who takes the cue*

54

*and also begins to smile. Valerian turns towards the other occupants of the car and starts to chuckle. Relieved, they start to chuckle too. For a split second, Mrs Thornhill is astonished at the effect of her remark. Then she too joins in the laughter. By now the laughter has built to a crescendo and the whole car is laughing, even the operator. In the center of all this stands a glowering Thornhill. The elevator comes to a stop.*

OPERATOR
Lobby, please. Watch your step.

*Thornhill's expression immediately changes to one of furtive calculation. We hear the sound of the elevator door opening and the outside lobby lights appear on his face. Valerian and Licht start to move out.*

THORNHILL
(*to both of them, politely*)
Excuse me. Ladies first, if you don't mind.

INT. LOBBY

*Camera is shooting into the elevator. Thornhill turns and starts backing out of the car as he ushers the ladies out. The ladies, in pushing their way out, ease Valerian and Licht towards the rear. As Thornhill backs away, the camera also retreats with him, but goes faster than he does. Thornhill is now far enough out to turn towards the camera and start running towards the 59th Street entrance, the camera panning with him.*

INT. LOBBY – ANOTHER ANGLE

*Thornhill is now running towards the camera. Behind him we see Valerian and Licht pushing their way between the women, and just in front of them, Mrs Thornhill, who is calling out:*

MRS THORNHILL
Roger – will you be home for dinner?

*Thornhill dashes out of the shot.*

EXT. PLAZA HOTEL

*A man and woman are waiting for a taxi, which is just pulling up. As the doorman opens the door for them, Thornhill comes dashing out of the*

55

*hotel, runs down the steps and jumps into the cab, past the astonished people. He slams the door shut and the cab starts to move off.*

INT. CAB

DRIVER

Where to?

THORNHILL

I don't know. Just keep going.

*The Driver shrugs. Thornhill turns, looks out of the back window. Over his shoulder we see Valerian and Licht dashing across the sidewalk and past the same startled couple and doorman into the next cab, which has just pulled up. Thornhill turns away, realizing he is still being followed, ponders the situation, then reaches into his pocket, takes out the torn newspaper photograph he had found in the hotel room and glances down at it thoughtfully. He looks up at the cab-driver.*

THORNHILL

Take me to the United Nations.

DRIVER

Right.

THORNHILL

The General Assembly Building.

DRIVER

Right.

THORNHILL

I'm being followed. Can you do something about it?

DRIVER

Yes. I can.

THORNHILL

Do it.

*The cab surges forward with a burst of speed.*

DISSOLVE TO:

## EXT. UNITED NATIONS HEADQUARTERS – DAY

*As seen from the north, a long high-angle shot showing the General Assembly building in the foreground, the 39-story marble and glass Secretariat building beyond it and, in the background, the East River and the Brooklyn skyline. At the extreme right, a taxicab is seen pulling up at the curb near the main entrance to the General Assembly building.*

## ENTRANCE. GENERAL ASSEMBLY BUILDING

CLOSE ANGLE: *Thornhill gets out of the cab, goes into the building.*

## INT. LOBBY. GENERAL ASSEMBLY BUILDING

*Thornhill crosses to the information desk. There are two girls stationed behind the desk, one of them a lovely Indian. She smiles at Thornhill.*

> GIRL
> May I help you, sir?

> THORNHILL
> Yes. Where would I find Mr Lester Townsend?

> GIRL
> *(writing on a pad)*
> Mr Townsend of UNIPO. And did you have an appointment, sir?

> THORNHILL
> I . . . uh . . . yes . . . uh . . . he expects me.

> GIRL
> Your name, sir?

> THORNHILL
> *(hesitates)*
> My name?

> GIRL
> Yes, please.

> THORNHILL
> Kaplan. George Kaplan.

One moment, please.

*She picks up a phone, starts to dial. Thornhill glances back towards the entrance door nervously.*

### EXT. STREET NEAR MAIN ENTRANCE

*Another cab is seen pulling up to the curb. Valerian gets out and, addressing Licht inside, gestures as though telling him to have the cab wait across the street. As the cab pulls away Valerian starts up the steps to the main entrance of the General Assembly building.*

### INT. LOBBY

*Thornhill is now receiving a slip of paper from the Girl at the information desk, who is saying:*

#### GIRL

. . . If you will give this to one of the attendants in the Public Lounge she will page him for you.

#### THORNHILL

Thank you very much.

#### GIRL

You're welcome, Mr Kaplan.

*Thornhill starts past the desk.*

### EXT. MAIN ENTRANCE

*Valerian crosses the courtyard and starts through the main doors.*

### INT. LOBBY

*Valerian enters and glances about. Then he walks in the direction of the information desk.*

### INT. PUBLIC LOUNGE

*Thornhill is just approaching the lounge. We enter with him, see the vast, high-ceilinged room with its high windows along the north wall looking out on the East River and the Queensboro Bridge in the*

*distance. The lounge is crowded with delegates of all nations; there are
many races, many different modes of dress. They sit on leather chairs
and sofas sipping tea, or stand in small conversational groups with
cocktails in hand. Others congregate at the bar at the east end of the
room. Everywhere is the buzz of many different tongues. And over it,
the Continuing Sound of the Public Address System as three pretty
attendants seated behind microphones near the telephone switchboard
send out their calls:*

VOICES OVER PA SYSTEM
'Miss Knox of Ceylon . . . United States Secretary please . . .
Mr Mahdi, delegation of Pakistan, please call the Public
Lounge . . . Mr Craig of the Secretariat, kindly call your
office . . . Mr Bernatti of the Swiss Observers Office . . . Mr
Bernatti of the Swiss Observers Office . . .'

*Thornhill goes up to one of the attendants (a 26-year-old American
girl), hands her the slip of paper.*

THORNHILL
Will you page Mr Lester Townsend, please?

ATTENDANT
(*consulting the slip*)
Certainly, Mr Kaplan.

*She picks up the microphone. We hear her voice over the PA system.*

Mr Townsend of UNIPO . . . Mr Townsend of UNIPO . . .
Please call at the communications desk of the Public Lounge.

*Thornhill stands gazing about the crowded room waiting for Townsend
to appear. Deep in background we see Valerian enter. He stops as he
sees Thornhill. There is a constant stream of activity at the
communications desk. Several different people emerge from the throng to
walk over to the desk. Thornhill pays them no attention, for none of
them is the man he is seeking. Finally one caller – a distinguished-
looking gentleman of about sixty – leans over and speaks to the
attendant, who then glances at Thornhill.*

ATTENDANT
Mr Kaplan . . .

THORNHILL
(*turning*)

Yes?

ATTENDANT
You wished to see Mr Townsend.

THORNHILL
Yes.

ATTENDANT
(*pointing*)
This is Mr Townsend.

*Thornhill looks at the strange man, blinks with puzzlement.*

TOWNSEND
How do you do, Mr Kaplan?

*He extends his hand.*

THORNHILL
(*to attendant*)
This isn't Mr Townsend.

TOWNSEND
(*smiling*)

Yes it is.

*He holds out his hand again. Thornhill shakes it dumbly.*

THORNHILL
There must be . . . some . . . mistake. *Lester* Townsend?

TOWNSEND
(*cheerfully*)
That's me.
(*as they stroll towards the windows*)
What can I do for you?

THORNHILL
(*still utterly bewildered*)
You're the Townsend who lives in Glen Cove?

TOWNSEND
That's right. Are we neighbors?

60

THORNHILL

A large red-brick house with a curving tree-lined driveway?

TOWNSEND
(smiles)

That's the one.

*As they walk across the room, they pass a press photographer taking flashbulb shots of a West African group.*

THORNHILL

Mr Townsend, were you at home last night?

TOWNSEND

You mean in Glen Cove?

THORNHILL

Yes.

TOWNSEND

No. I've been staying in my apartment in town for the past month. Always do when we're in session here.

THORNHILL

What about *Mrs* Townsend?

TOWNSEND
(frowns)

My wife has been dead for many years.
(*Thornhill stares at him*)
Look here, Mr Kaplan, what's this all about?

THORNHILL

Who are those people living in your house?

TOWNSEND

What people? The house is completely closed up. There's just a gardener and his wife living on the grounds. Now, Mr Kaplan – suppose you tell me who you are and what you want.

*Thornhill takes the newspaper photograph from his pocket, starts to show it to Townsend.*

THORNHILL
Do you know this man?

*Townsend glances at the picture, then suddenly gasps and utters a strangled cry. His eyes widen and he sags against Thornhill, who puts his arms around him automatically to support him.*

Here. What's wrong?

*Townsend groans. His eyes flutter. Thornhill's right hand closes on the handle of a knife protruding from Townsend's back. Instinctively, he grasps the knife, pulls it out. Townsend slumps to the floor, dead. Thornhill stands there in horror staring down at him, the bloody knife in his upraised hand. It has all happened so swiftly that nobody has actually seen the slaying. Valerian is seen hurrying away. A woman's voice is heard crying out: 'Look!' A man's voice shouts: 'What happened?' Thornhill looks up, sees a circle of horrified, angry faces staring at him. A woman points at him accusingly: 'He did it! I saw him!' The group moves towards him slowly, threateningly. Another voice cries out: 'Look out! He's got a knife!' Thornhill backs away slowly, dazed and confused.*

Wait a minute now . . . Listen to me . . . I had nothing to do with this . . .

VOICES
*(overlapping)*
Somebody do something! . . . I saw him! . . . Call the police! . . . Grab him! . . .

THORNHILL
*(frightened)*
Don't come any nearer! Get back!

*There is a click and a flash of light. The press photographer has whipped his camera around and caught a perfect shot of the stunned Thornhill backing away from the fallen body with the bloody knife still clenched threateningly in his hand. Panic on his face, he drops the knife and flees from the room before the startled onlookers can make a move.*

DISSOLVE TO:

INT. CONFERENCE ROOM. CENTRAL INTELLIGENCE AGENCY.
WASHINGTON, DC – EARLY EVENING

*Start close on front page of a Washington evening paper featuring the
incriminating photo of Thornhill in his 'killer's' pose; above it, screamer
headlines:* 'DIPLOMAT SLAIN AT UN; ASSASSIN ELUDES POLICE'. *A
man's voice is heard over the shot reading aloud what is obviously part
of the news story. During this we pull back to reveal a group of four men
and one woman seated around a conference table. As the camera leaves
the insert of the newspaper and starts its rise, we also catch a glimpse of
official documents on which we see the words:* 'TOP SECRET'.

> MAN'S VOICE
> (reading)
> . . . The photograph has been tentatively identified as that of
> Roger Thornhill, a Manhattan advertising executive,
> indicating that the name George Kaplan, which he gave to an
> attendant in the General Assembly Building, was false. A
> possible motive for the slaying was suggested by the discovery
> that earlier today, Thornhill appeared in a Glen Cove, Long
> Island, police court on a charge of drunk driving with a stolen

car, and in his defense charged that the murder victim, Mr Townsend, had attempted to kill *him* the night before . . .

*The man puts the newspaper down on the table, looks up at the other people. Their ages vary from thirty-five to fifty; there is nothing about an Intelligence agent's appearance that distinguishes them from, say, a college professor or a stockbroker or a reporter or a housewife. These people happen to be all of that, too. The gentleman who has been reading the newspaper, for example, is, among other things, a limner of comic cartoons for the national magazines.*

CARTOONIST

Brother . . .

STOCKBROKER

What about that?

HOUSEWIFE

Does anybody *know* this Thornhill?

CARTOONIST

Not me.

STOCKBROKER

Never heard of him.

HOUSEWIFE

Professor?

*The Professor shakes his head negatively.*

REPORTER

Apparently the poor sucker got mistaken for George Kaplan.

CARTOONIST

How could he be mistaken for George Kaplan when George Kaplan doesn't even exist?

REPORTER

Don't ask me how it happened, but obviously it happened. Vandamm's men must have grabbed him and tried to put him away, using Lester Townsend's house.

STOCKBROKER
(*nodding*)

And the unsuspecting Townsend winds up with a stray knife
in his back.

REPORTER
(*shrugs*)

*C'est la guerre.*

CARTOONIST
(*shaking his head*)

It's so horribly sad. Why is it I feel like laughing?

HOUSEWIFE

Never mind *that*. What are we going to do?

CARTOONIST

Do?

HOUSEWIFE

About Mr Thornhill . . .

STOCKBROKER

Good question.

*They look at each other uncertainly. Finally the mildest mannered of
them all, the College Professor, speaks up quietly, enunciating with
elaborate preciseness.*

PROFESSOR

We do . . . nothing.

HOUSEWIFE

Nothing?

PROFESSOR
(*getting up*)

That's right . . . nothing.
(*with a gesture*)

Oh, we *could* congratulate ourselves on a marvelous stroke of
good fortune . . .
(*he meets their puzzled stares with a delighted announcement*)

Our non-existent decoy, George Kaplan – created to divert

65

suspicion from our own Number One – has fortuitously
become a *live* decoy.

**HOUSEWIFE**

Yes, Professor. And how long do you think he's going to *stay*
live?

**PROFESSOR**

That's *his* problem.

**STOCKBROKER**

What Mrs Finley means –

**PROFESSOR**
(*amused*)

I know what she means.

**STOCKBROKER**

– We can't just sit back calmly and wait to see who kills him
first . . . Vandamm and company or the police.

**PROFESSOR**
(*forcefully*)

There's nothing we can do to save him without endangering
Number One!

**HOUSEWIFE**

Aren't we being just a wee bit callous?

*The Professor's tolerant attitude vanishes.*

**PROFESSOR**

No, my dear woman, we are *not* being callous. We did not
invent our non-existent man, and establish elaborate
behaviour patterns for him, and move his prop belongings in
and out of hotel rooms, for our *own private amusement*. We
created George Kaplan and labored to convince Vandamm
that this phantom was our own Number One, hot on his trail,
for a *desperately important reason*.

**REPORTER**

Check.

66

**STOCKBROKER**

Nobody's denying that.

**PROFESSOR**
(*passionately*)

All right then. If we make the slightest move to suggest that
there *is* no such agent as George Kaplan . . . give *any* hint to
Vandamm that he's pursuing a *decoy* instead of our real
Number One . . . then Number One, working right under
Vandamm's nose, will immediately face suspicion, exposure
and assassination, like the two others who went before.

*There is a moment of embarrassed silence around the table as they all
realize the unpleasant truth of what the Professor has just said.*

**HOUSEWIFE**
(*softly, sadly*)

Goodbye, Mr Thornhill . . . wherever you are.

DISSOLVE TO:

**INT. GRAND CENTRAL STATION. NYC – EARLY EVENING**
*Shooting from a high vantage point, we disclose the vast, bustling main
lobby of the terminal. Police are seen entering from the 42nd Street side –
two lieutenants in uniform and two plain-clothes detectives. They look
about, come to a stop, confer and then disperse. Camera pans slightly to
a phone booth. We see Thornhill inside, talking on the phone.*

**INT. PHONE BOOTH**

**THORNHILL**
(*exasperated*)

But, Mother, I *called* the Plaza. Kaplan checked out and went
to the Ambassador East in Chicago. That's why I'm –
(*he listens impatiently*)
I *can't* go to the police. Not yet. *You* saw the newspapers. My
fingerprints are on the knife; I'm a drunk driver, a car thief
and I murdered a man for revenge. I wouldn't have a chance,
and I *won't* have until I find George Kaplan, who obviously
knows what this is all about.
(*listens again*)

67

No, the train. It's safer.
>                    (*another interruption*)
Because there's no room to hide on a plane if someone
should recognize me. You want me to jump off a moving
plane?
>                    (*nods, then with angry sarcasm*)
Thank you so much, Mother.

*There is a loud clatter as Mrs Thornhill hangs up on him. Thornhill
stares at the receiver a moment, then hangs up and pushes out of the
booth.*

INT. TERMINAL

*As he emerges from the booth, he comes face to face with a large man
who could be a detective. For a brief, tense moment they stare at each
other, and then the man steps past him into the booth. Thornhill looks
about cautiously, then starts walking across the lobby towards the ticket
windows, camera moving with him. Near the information booth, a man
stands reading the center pages of the NY Post. Thornhill sees the front
page headlines: 'MANHUNT ON FOR UN KILLER'. This reminds him to
take out dark glasses and put them on, which he does as he continues
across the lobby and steps up to a Pullman ticket window. A Ticket
Agent moves up to him, peers at the dark glasses.*

>                    AGENT
Yes?

>                    THORNHILL
Give me a bedroom or whatever you got on the Twentieth
Century.

>                    AGENT
>                    (*slowly*)
Leaving in five minutes.

>                    THORNHILL
>                    (*impatiently*)
I know. Come on.

>                    AGENT
I think they're all sold out.

THORNHILL

Sold out?

AGENT

You can always go coach.

THORNHILL

No, I . . . I can't. When's the next train?

AGENT

Nothing till ten.
(*peering at him*)
You're in a hurry, huh?

THORNHILL
(*sharply*)
Call them and see what you can do.

AGENT
(*still peering*)
Something wrong with your eyes?

THORNHILL

Yes. They're sensitive to questions. Will you *call* them?

AGENT
(*still staring at him*)
Sure . . . sure . . .

REVERSE ANGLE: TICKET OFFICE
*We are behind the agent, shooting through the window opening on Thornhill. What we see (and Thornhill cannot) is that the agent is now looking down at a glossy photograph of Thornhill with knife in hand, obviously a police department copy of the original. He glances up at Thornhill again.*

AGENT

Don't go away.

*The agent walks away from the window, camera moving with him. Out of Thornhill's line of sight in the rear of the ticket office, he picks up a phone, dials three times, waits, then –*
(*softly, into phone*)

69

He's at Window Fifteen, upper-level. Hurry.

*He hangs up, swallows nervously, composes himself, steps to the ticket rack, takes down a ticket, returns to the window saying airily:*

You're in luck, mister –

*He stops, stares. Nobody is at the window. He leans through, peers about. Thornhill is gone.*

LONG SHOT: THE TERMINAL
*Thornhill has withdrawn to a vantage point across the lobby. In distant background the agent is seen pulling his head back in. In close foreground, Thornhill stands watching him, hidden by the intervening crowds. Now he sees two men – the police lieutenants – hurrying up to the ticket window, conferring with the agent, then turning, looking about.*

ANOTHER ANGLE
*Thornhill turns away, moves swiftly towards the train platform entrances, camera dollying with him. He sees the sign above Track 29:*
TWENTIETH CENTURY LIMITED. *He starts through the gate. A Guard stops him.*

GUARD

Ticket?

THORNHILL

I . . . uh . . . I'm just seeing some friends off.

*He starts through. The Guard grabs him.*

GUARD

Sorry. I'll have to know their name and space before I can let you through.

*Thornhill looks back, sees the police running across the lobby towards the gate. He yanks his arm free, pushes the Guard aside, goes through the gate and runs past the desk where train officials are verifying passenger space.*

## EXT. THE PLATFORM

### GUARD'S VOICE
#### (off-screen)
Wait a minute! Come back here!

*Thornhill continues to run, camera moving with him. In background, the police reach the gate, confer with the Guard. As Thornhill reaches the rear car of the waiting train, he turns, looks back. The police are coming after him. Up and down the platform, porters are calling out: 'All Aboard!' Thornhill quickly boards the train.*

## INT. TRAIN

*Thornhill hurries through a car, looks out of the window, takes his dark glasses off and sees the police running along the platform to enter the car up ahead. He turns, starts back. Another passenger is approaching. It is a lovely, smartly-dressed Girl of twenty-six. Thornhill tries to get past her. The aisle is narrow. She steps to one side. But he steps to the same side. He moves to the other side – just as she does.*

### GIRL
Sorry.

### THORNHILL
My fault.

*They move to the center – but in unison. Again an impasse.*

Sorry.

### GIRL
My fault.

*Meanwhile, the police have boarded the train. Thornhill and the girl are getting nowhere, just blocking each other. The police come into view at the other end of the car. Momentarily distracted by an outgoing Redcap, they haven't spotted Thornhill yet. The Girl sees the men, notices their uniforms, senses Thornhill's urgency. Thornhill catches her look, ducks into an open compartment filled with luggage but no passenger as yet, and pulls the door partially closed. The police come running through the car.*

71

                    GIRL
                  (*pointing*)
He went that way. I think he got off.

*They follow her directions, continue on. The compartment door opens,*
*Thornhill steps out, sees the coast is clear.*

                  THORNHILL
Thank you very much.

                    GIRL
Quite all right.

                  THORNHILL
                  (*lamely*)
Seven parking tickets.

                    GIRL
Oh.

*She walks away. He looks after her. The view is quite attractive. The*
*train starts moving. He peers out of the window.*

EXT. THE PLATFORM

*The police have been searching the platform. They turn, watch helplessly*
*as the train pulls away.*

    DISSOLVE TO:

EXT. NY CENTRAL TRACKS – NIGHT

*Somewhere along the Hudson River, the Twentieth Century Limited*
*comes around a bend, speeds towards camera and races by.*

INT. CLUB CAR

*A Pullman Conductor and his assistant are finishing up the business of*
*collecting tickets and verifying Pullman space. They move through the*
*car, studying the passengers who sit there reading magazines and*
*newspapers, recognizing most of them as having handed over their*
*tickets earlier. There is doubt about one passenger, an elderly woman.*

72

CONDUCTOR

Do I have your ticket, madam?

WOMAN

Why yes. I gave it to you an hour ago.

CONDUCTOR

And that space was . . . ?

WOMAN

Bedroom F. in Car eighteen-oh-one.

CONDUCTOR<br>(consulting his chart)

Thank you.

WOMAN<br>(a little huffy)

You're welcome.

*The Conductor and his Assistant continue on until they come to a door labelled: 'WASHROOM'. The Assistant tries the handle, finds the door unlocked, opens it slightly and peers in. Satisfied that the washroom is unoccupied, he closes the door, and the two men continue on.*

*After a moment, the washroom door opens, Thornhill peers out, then emerges and moves off in the opposite direction through the club car. As he passes a table, he sees an evening paper lying there with his own picture on the front page, face up. He stops, casually turns the paper over, and continues on towards the dining car.*

INT. DINING CAR

*As Thornhill enters from the next car, the Steward approaches him.*

STEWARD

Good evening, sir. One?

THORNHILL

Please.

*The Steward leads him into the dining area. It is fairly crowded. The Girl is there, seated alone at a table for two. She is on dessert and coffee. Without a word, the Steward leads Thornhill directly to her table and*

73

*pulls out the chair for him. The Girl looks up at Thornhill, smiles fleetingly. He returns the smile and sits down.*

STEWARD

Cocktail before dinner?

THORNHILL

How about a Gibson?

STEWARD

Right away.

*He goes off. Thornhill takes up the menu, studies it. The Girl raises her eyes, studies him. He looks up, catches her glance. She quickly looks down. He glances down at the menu again, then looks up at her. She glances up, catches him, and he looks away. Now she looks away. Then they both look up at each other at the same time and meet head on. They smile.*

THORNHILL

Well – here we are again.

GIRL

Yes.

THORNHILL
*(looking down at menu)*

Recommend anything?

GIRL

The brook trout. A little 'trouty' but quite good.

THORNHILL

Sold.

*He writes out the order. A waiter brings his Gibson, takes the order and leaves. Thornhill glances about the dining car nervously, sees (or perhaps imagines he sees) several people staring at him. When he looks back at the Girl, he finds that she is scrutinizing him.*

I know. I look vaguely familiar to you.

GIRL

Yes.

74

**THORNHILL**

You feel you've seen me somewhere before.

**GIRL**

Yes.

**THORNHILL**

Funny how I have that effect on people wherever I go.
Something about my face . . .

**GIRL**

It's a nice face.

**THORNHILL**

You really think so?

**GIRL**

I would never say it if I didn't.

**THORNHILL**

Oh – you're *that* type.

**GIRL**

What type?

**THORNHILL**

Honest.

**GIRL**

Not really.

**THORNHILL**

Good. Honest women frighten me.

**GIRL**

Why?

**THORNHILL**

I feel at a disadvantage with them.

**GIRL**

Because *you're* not honest with *them*.

**THORNHILL**

Exactly.

**GIRL**

Like that business about the seven parking tickets . . .

**THORNHILL**
(*stepping delicately past it*)

What I mean is: the moment I meet an attractive girl, I have to start pretending that I've no desire to make love to her.

**GIRL**

What makes you think you have to conceal it?

**THORNHILL**

She might find the idea objectionable.

**GIRL**
(*provocatively*)

And then again, she might not.

**THORNHILL**

Think how lucky I am to have been seated here.

**GIRL**

Luck had nothing to do with it.

**THORNHILL**

Fate?

**GIRL**

I tipped the steward five dollars to seat you here if you should come in.

*Thornhill looks at her for a long moment.*

**THORNHILL**

Is that a proposition?

*She looks right back at him for an equally long moment.*

**GIRL**

I never make love on an empty stomach.

**THORNHILL**

You've already eaten.

**GIRL**

But you haven't.

*They continue to gaze at each other, and then the waiter brings dinner
and sets it on the table. Thornhill goes to work on it.*

THORNHILL

Don't you think it's time we were introduced?

GIRL

I'm Eve Kendall. Twenty-six and unmarried. Now you know
everything.

THORNHILL

What do you do besides lure men to their doom on the New
York Central?

EVE

I'm an industrial designer.

THORNHILL

Jack Phillips. Western sales manager of Kingby Electronics.

EVE
*(easily)*

No you're not. You're Roger Thornhill of Madison Avenue
and you're wanted for murder on every front page in
America. Don't be so modest.

THORNHILL

Oops.

EVE

Don't worry. I won't say a word.

THORNHILL

How come?

EVE

I told you – it's a nice face.

THORNHILL

Is that the only reason?

EVE
*(shrugs)*

It's going to be a long night . . .

THORNHILL
(*nods*)

True.

EVE

And I don't particularly like the book I've started . . .

THORNHILL

Ah.

EVE

You know what I mean?

THORNHILL

Oh – exactly.

*Eve puts a cigarette between her lips, looks quite boldly into Thornhill's eyes as he takes a folder of matches from his pocket. She notices the match folder, takes it from him and examines it. (We will see it in an insert.) On each side of the folder, three large letters: ROT.*
(*explaining*)

My trademark – rot.

EVE

Roger O. Thornhill. What's the O. for?

THORNHILL

Nothing.

*He strikes a match to light her cigarette. (Meanwhile, the train has been slowing down as it approaches a station.) She takes his hand in hers and guides the flame to her cigarette, her hands lingering on his with an unmistakable intimacy that he finds downright delightful.*

I'd invite you to my bedroom if I had a bedroom.

EVE

Roomette?

THORNHILL

Nothing – not even a ticket. I've been playing hide-and-seek with the Pullman conductor ever since we left New York.

EVE

How awkward for you.

THORNHILL

No place to sleep.

EVE

I've got a large drawing-room all to myself.

THORNHILL

That's not fair, is it?

EVE

Drawing-room E, car thirty-nine-oh-one.

THORNHILL

A nice number.

EVE

Easy to remember.

THORNHILL

Thirty-nine-oh-one.

EVE

See?

> THORNHILL

I have no luggage.

> EVE
> (*looking out of the window*)

So?

> THORNHILL

You wouldn't happen to have an extra pair of pajamas, would you?

*She looks him right in the eye.*

> EVE

Wouldn't I?

*Then she puts money on her tab and gets to her feet, as Thornhill stares up at her, slightly awed. The train comes to a stop.*

Incidentally, I wouldn't order any dessert if I were you.

> THORNHILL
> (*pats his stomach*)

I get the message.

> EVE

That wasn't quite what I meant. The train seems to be making an unscheduled stop, and I just saw two men getting out of a police car as we pulled into the station. They weren't smiling.

*She walks away, and Thornhill looks out of the window. Two Detectives are seen hurrying along the platform to board the train. Thornhill puts some money on the table, gets to his feet and saunters out of the car in the direction Eve has taken. Camera pans quickly to the other end of the car, picks up the two Detectives entering the dining area and looking about. The Steward walks up to them, as the train starts moving again.*

DISSOLVE TO:

*Eve is seated by the window with a book in her lap, apparently alone. Thornhill is nowhere to be seen. Sometime during the scene, the camera will indicate to us that his muffled voice is coming from behind the closed upper berth, where he is locked in. Eve continues to glance at her book as she speaks.*

> THORNHILL'S VOICE

I think you better go out and tell those police to hurry.

> EVE

Patience is a virtue.

> THORNHILL'S VOICE

So is breathing.

> EVE

Just lie still.

> THORNHILL'S VOICE

Do you have any olive oil?

> EVE

Olive oil?

> THORNHILL'S VOICE

I want to be packed in olive oil if I'm going to be a sardine.

*The door buzzer sounds. Eve remains seated, calls out in a loud voice:*

> EVE

Come in.

*The door opens. The dining-car Steward is seen in the corridor. He looks in at Eve, speaks apologetically.*

> STEWARD

I'm sorry to disturb you. Some gentlemen here would like to have a word with you.

> MAN'S VOICE
> *(off-screen)*

Okay. Thanks.

*The Steward goes off, and the two Detectives enter.*

Your name, please?

EVE

Eve Kendall. Who are you?

FIRST DETECTIVE
(*showing identification*)

State Police.

EVE

Is anything wrong?

*Meanwhile, the Second Detective is opening the closet door and the lavatory door and peering into every nook and cranny of the drawing-room.*

FIRST DETECTIVE

There was a man seated at your table tonight in the dining car.

EVE

Yes.

FIRST DETECTIVE

Friend of yours?

EVE

I never saw him before.

FIRST DETECTIVE

This the man?

*He hands her a photograph. She takes it, studies it.*

EVE

Why yes. I think so. It's not a very clear picture.

FIRST DETECTIVE

It's a wire photo. We just got it from the New York police.

EVE

Police?

FIRST DETECTIVE

He's wanted for murder.

82

**EVE**

*(getting up)*

Good heavens. No.

**FIRST DETECTIVE**

We thought maybe he was in here with you.

**EVE**

With me? I told you, I don't even know the man.

**FIRST DETECTIVE**

The steward said you left the dining car together.

**EVE**

We might have happened to *leave* at the same time but not together.

**FIRST DETECTIVE**

What did you two talk about?

**EVE**

Talk about?

**FIRST DETECTIVE**

Yeah. Your waiter said you were getting along pretty good with this Thornhill fellow.

**EVE**

Is that his name – Thornhill?

**FIRST DETECTIVE**

Didn't he tell you?

**EVE**

No. Didn't tell me anything. All we did was chat . . . about different kinds of food . . . train travel versus plane travel . . . that sort of thing . . . rather innocuous, I must say, considering that he was a fugitive from justice. Who did he kill?

**FIRST DETECTIVE**

He didn't say where he was going, did he?

**EVE**

No – I assumed Chicago. You think perhaps he got off when you got on?

83

FIRST DETECTIVE
(*rather grimly*)
Look - if you happen to catch sight of him again, Miss . . . uh –

EVE
Kendall.

FIRST DETECTIVE
. . . Will you let us know?

EVE
I'm going to bed soon, and I intend to lock my door, so I doubt if I'll be seeing him or anybody else tonight.

FIRST DETECTIVE
Well just in case you do – we'll be in the observation car at the rear of the train.

EVE
It's comforting to know that.

*Disgruntled, the two men walk out.*

Good night.

*She closes the door, goes quickly to her handbag as she says:*

Still breathing?

THORNHILL'S VOICE
(*pleading weakly*)
Either hurry, or bring me a snorkel.

EVE
(*fumbling in her bag*)
I'm looking for that can opener I stole from the porter.

*She takes out the key-like device which porters use to open Pullman beds. She inserts it in the lock, turns it, and the upper berth crashes open, bouncing Thornhill into view.*

Hello there.

*He sits up, heaves a sigh of relief, removes his sun-glasses from his pocket and stares sourly at them. They are smashed. He drops the pieces on the bed, then looks down at Eve and smiles with friendly puzzlement.*

84

(during above)
All clear.

THORNHILL
Why are you so good to me?

*She gazes up at him and smiles.*

EVE
Shall I climb up and tell you why?

EXT. TRAIN – LONG SHOT
*As it speeds through the darkness.*

CLOSE SHOT: THE DIESEL LOCOMOTIVE
*As its horn blasts four times.*

DISSOLVE TO:

INT. EVE'S DRAWING-ROOM – LATER

*The upper berth is closed now. Eve and Thornhill are standing close
together in the dark murmuring to each other between frequent kisses.
We hear them more than see them, for they are revealed to us only by
the passing lights outside the windows. Her back is against the wall near
the light switches. He is standing directly in front of her, his hands at her
waist. Her hands are at his shoulders, not helping, not resisting.*

EVE
You know, I've been thinking – it's not safe for you to roam
around Chicago looking for this George Kaplan you've been
telling me about. You'll be picked up by the police the
moment you show your face . . .

THORNHILL
(*kissing her*)
And it's such a nice face, too.

EVE
(*kissing him back*)
Don't you think it would be better if you stayed in my hotel
room while *I* located Mr Kaplan and brought him to you?

85

**THORNHILL**

Can't let you get involved. Too dangerous.

**EVE**

I'm a big girl.

**THORNHILL**
(*nibbling away*)

In all the right places, too.

**EVE**
(*responding with growing excitement*)

This is ridiculous. You *know* that, don't you?

**THORNHILL**
(*kissing her lips*)

Yes.

**EVE**

I mean, we've hardly *met*.

**THORNHILL**

That's right.

**EVE**

How do I know you *aren't* a murderer?

**THORNHILL**
(*to her neck*)

You don't.

**EVE**

Maybe you're planning to murder *me*, right here, tonight.

**THORNHILL**
(*working on her ear*)

Shall I?

**EVE**
(*whispers*)

Yes . . . please do . . .

*This time her hands do help him, and it is a long kiss indeed.*

THORNHILL

What's happening to us?

EVE

We're just strangers on a train.

THORNHILL

Beats flying, doesn't it?

EVE

We should stop.

THORNHILL
(*continuing*)

Immediately.

EVE

I ought to know more about you.

THORNHILL
(*kissing her*)

The rest is unimportant.

EVE

You're an advertising man, that's all I know. You've got taste in clothes . . . taste in food –

THORNHILL

Taste in women.
(*tasting her*)

I like your flavor.

EVE

And you're very clever with words. You can probably make them do anything for you . . . Sell people things they don't need . . . Make women who don't know you fall in love with you . . .

THORNHILL

I'm beginning to think I'm underpaid.

*And then they come together slowly in a long kiss that might never have ended if the door buzzer hadn't sounded. They break apart, look towards the door. Thornhill quickly steps inside the lavatory and closes*

*the door, as Eve snaps on the overhead lights, goes to the other door,*
*unlocks it and opens it. A Porter is standing there.*

EVE
(*for Thornhill's ears*)
Oh – the porter. I suppose you want to make up my bed.

PORTER
(*entering*)
Yes, ma'am.

EVE
(*holding up the key*)
Is this yours? I found it on the floor.

PORTER
Why yes, ma'am. I've been looking all over for it.

*As the Porter opens a lower berth and starts making up the bed, Eve*
*takes up her handbag and says, for Thornhill's benefit:*

EVE
I'll wait outside.

*She starts to open her handbag as she goes out to the corridor.*

INT. LAVATORY

*Thornhill is looking at his face in the mirror and feeling his chin. He*
*looks around at Eve's toiletries, sees a tiny ladies' safety razor and a*
*tiny shaving brush. He picks the razor up and looks from it to himself in*
*the mirror with blank expression. He gives a casual half turn as he hears*
*the voices of Eve and the Porter.*

EVE'S VOICE
Thank you, porter.

PORTER'S VOICE
Thank *you*, ma'am. Good night now.

EVE'S VOICE
Good night.

*Then he hears the compartment door being closed and locked, and a*
*knock on the lavatory door.*

Come out, come out, wherever you are.

*Thornhill opens the door and steps out.*

INT. DRAWING-ROOM

> EVE
> (*by way of explanation*)

The porter . . .

> THORNHILL
> (*noticing the open bed*)

Uh huh . . .

> (*he snaps off the overhead lights*)

Now where were we?

> EVE
> (*moving close*)

Here?

> THORNHILL
> (*holding her*)

Ah.

*They kiss.*

> (*murmurs*)
I see he opened the bed.

#### EVE

Yes . . .

#### THORNHILL

Only one bed.

#### EVE

Yes . . .

#### THORNHILL

I think it's a good omen. Don't you?

#### EVE
> (*sighs*)

Wonderful.

#### THORNHILL

Know what it means?

#### EVE
> (*dreamily*)

Mmm.

#### THORNHILL
> (*softly*)

Tell me.

#### EVE

It means . . . that *you* . . .
> (*she looks up at him*)
. . . are going to sleep on the floor . . .

*He gives her a look.*

#### THORNHILL

Here. Take your omen back.

*Eve kisses him gently on the lips, and as she presses her cheek against his, her expression sobers for a moment and her eyes turn to the door thoughtfully.*

**INT. TRAIN — ANOTHER CAR**

*Shooting down the corridor, we see the Porter moving away from us. In his right hand is a folded piece of white paper.*

**CLOSER ANGLE: SIDE VIEW OF PORTER**
*The camera is now travelling with him. When he comes to a stop before the door of a drawing-room, the camera continues to travel a bit while he presses the buzzer. Camera is now facing the Porter. The door opens. We do not see the occupant.*

> **PORTER**
> (*holding out the piece of paper*)
> A message from the lady in car thirty-nine-oh-one.

*A man's hand emerges and takes the note. The Porter turns and moves away.*

**INT. DRAWING-ROOM**

*The man's hands unfold the note and it fills the screen. It says:*

> What do I do with him in the morning?
> [signed]
> Eve.

**FULL SHOT. DRAWING-ROOM**
*Leonard, the secretary of Glen Cove, is closing the door, turning and handing the note to his master, Phillip Vandamm, the man whom Thornhill had mistakenly assumed at Glen Cove to be Lester Townsend. Over this, the sound of the diesel horn blasting four times.*

FADE OUT:

FADE IN:

**INT. TRAIN PLATFORM — LA SALLE STREET STATION, CHICAGO — MORNING**

*The Twentieth Century Limited has come to the end of its run. Moving camera reveals passengers getting off, luggage being unloaded by Pullman porters, Redcaps swarming over the platform, some of them boarding the train, others getting off with luggage in hand. And now*

*camera picks up the two Detectives who boarded the train the night*
*before. They are conferring with other plain-clothesmen and uniformed*
*police who have come to meet the train. The men disperse, eyeing the*
*off-going passengers as they take up positions.*

ANOTHER ANGLE
*Eve is seen getting off the train. Behind her comes a Redcap carrying her*
*luggage. As we dolly with them along the long, crowded platform*
*towards the terminal, we see that,* beneath the red hat and the
uniform, the baggage-smasher is really Thornhill.

CLOSE SHOT: THE TWO DETECTIVES
*As they see Eve.*

POINT OF VIEW: FROM DETECTIVES
*Eve approaching, followed by her 'Redcap'.*

MOVING SHOT: THORNHILL AND EVE
*Eve sees the Detectives up ahead. She slows down, lets Thornhill draw*
*abreast of her as they walk.*

> EVE
> (*sotto voce*)
> Keep walking. I'll catch up.

> THORNHILL
> Yes, ma'am.

*The two Detectives step into her path. She stops. Thornhill continues on.*

> FIRST DETECTIVE
> Anything to report, Miss Kendall?

> EVE
> (*with enthusiasm*)
> Why yes. I had a *fine* night's sleep.

> FIRST DETECTIVE
> (*shaking his head with annoyance*)
> I mean did you happen to see the man we're looking for?

> **EVE**
Mr Thornycroft?

> **FIRST DETECTIVE**
Thornhill.

> **EVE**
Oh . . . No . . . I'm awfully sorry.
> (*she smiles*)
But good luck to you both.

*She walks away. The two Detectives look after her with sour expression.*

**MOVING SHOT: EVE AND THORNHILL**
*Eve catches up with her 'Redcap', moves abreast of him as he struggles with the heavy luggage.*

> **EVE**
How're we doing?

> **THORNHILL**
> (*exhausted*)
I may collapse any minute.

> **EVE**
Not yet. First we have to run the gauntlet. Look.

**MOVING POINT OF VIEW: FROM EVE AND THORNHILL**
*Police are lined up along the platform up ahead, eyeing everyone who passes.*

**MOVING SHOT: EVE AND THORNHILL**
*They move right along under the very eyes of the police, talking to each other with a technique that would arouse the approval of any ventriloquist:*

> **THORNHILL**
> (*sweating*)
I'm accustomed to having a load on . . . What *have* you got in these bags?

> **EVE**
Bowling balls – naturally.

THORNHILL

Which one of these has my suit in it?

EVE

The small zippered affair underneath your right arm.

THORNHILL

*That* ought to do it a lot of good.

EVE

I'm sure Mr Kaplan won't mind a few wrinkles.

THORNHILL

If he's still there. What time is it?

EVE

Nine-thirty.

THORNHILL

He may have left his hotel room by now.

EVE

I'll call him for you as soon as we get inside the station.

THORNHILL

No. I'll do it.

EVE

Redcap in a phone booth? Slightly suspicious.

THORNHILL

All right. You know what to tell him?

EVE

You want to see him right away. Terribly urgent. Matter of life and death. No explanations.

THORNHILL

Good.

EVE

And while I'm calling, you change your clothes.

THORNHILL

Where do you propose I do that – in Marshall Field's window?

EVE

I sort of had the Men's Room in mind.

THORNHILL
(*gives her a look*)
*Did* you now.
(*pause*)
You're the smartest girl I ever spent the night with on a train.

*She glances at him with a slight smile. He gives her a sour look.*

CLOSE-UP: EVE
*As she looks straight ahead again, her expression becomes thoughtful with a trace of distress. She turns her head slightly.*

EXT. PLATFORM

*In a medium shot, we now see the subject of Eve's troubled thoughts: Vandamm and Leonard, who are getting off their Pullman car. They start to walk towards the camera.*

CLOSE-UP: EVE
*She glances at Thornhill with a trace of sadness in her eyes.*

CLOSE-UP: THORNHILL (FROM EVE'S POINT OF VIEW)
*With a cheerful eye cocked for any signs of danger ahead.*

THE PLATFORM UP AHEAD (FROM THORNHILL'S POINT OF VIEW)
— MOVING SHOT
*There are no police in sight.*

TWO SHOT: THORNHILL AND EVE

THORNHILL
Looks like we've made it.

SEMI-LONG SHOT: THE PLATFORM
*There is a commotion around the steps of the car from which Eve and Thornhill alighted. On the top of the steps appears a hatless, middle-aged man in his underwear, socks and shoes. Behind him are two uniformed Policemen pushing him down the steps to the platform. Our*

*two Detectives quickly step forward to question him. At the same time,*
*the two uniformed Police alight to the platform and complete the small*
*knot of men surrounding the uniformless Redcap. For a moment we see*
*the hapless Redcap gesticulating as he describes how he came to be in*
*this state of undress. Then suddenly the Police and Detectives dash away*
*and down the platform towards the main lobby, leaving the man*
*standing there in his underwear.*

CLOSE SHOT: THE REDCAP
*He watches the departing police, then fishes out a few dollar bills from*
*inside his underwear and counts them over.*

INT. MAIN LOBBY – HIGH ANGLE SHOT

*Much activity, many people, a profusion of Redcaps. If one of them is*
*Thornhill, it is difficult to tell. Now we see the four minions of the law*
*arriving in the lobby. They dash about, rounding up Redcaps, who*
*submit to examination with much bewilderment. One Detective whips*
*off a Redcap's hat. Angrily the man snatches it back. Another Detective*
*spots a Redcap who is hurrying away, his back to camera. He looks*
*very much like Thornhill from the rear. The Detective grabs him, whirls*
*him around, and finds himself staring into a stunned, open mouthful of*
*teeth that definitely do not answer to the description of Thornhill's.*

INT. MEN'S ROOM

*There is considerable activity here. At the row of wash basins stand three*
*men. One is washing his hands, the other is scraping away at his chin*
*with a straight razor, and the third man – Thornhill – is busily rubbing*
*in a foamy lather which covers the lower half of his face. He is in his*
*regular trousers by now, and his jacket hangs nearby. At his feet stands*
*Eve's small zippered bag. The Redcap uniform is nowhere to be seen.*
*Suddenly the door bursts open and our two Detectives enter. Thornhill*
*and the other men turn at the commotion, casually watch the Detectives*
*glancing about in search of their quarry. As Thornhill turns back to the*
*mirror and continues to lather his face, we hear the sound of stall doors*
*opening and banging closed. Their mission unaccomplished, the*
*Detectives go out. Thornhill nonchalantly finishes his lathering, then*
*looks down and picks up his razor, which, up to now, we have not seen.*
*It is the tiny one belonging to Eve. He starts to draw it down his cheek,*

*leaving the narrowest of lines down the lather. Then in the mirror he
catches sight of the man with the straight razor staring at him in
bewilderment.*

### EXT. PHONE BOOTH IN MAIN LOBBY

*We see Eve through the glass doors, listening to someone on the phone,
writing on a memo pad and saying a few words of agreement. The
camera now begins to travel along the row of booths. We see various
people at telephones. The camera comes to a stop outside another booth.
Through the glass we see Leonard speaking. He seems to be issuing
specific instructions, glances at his wrist-watch once. After a pause, he
hangs up.*

### EXT. ROW OF BOOTHS

*A raking shot of the line of booths, showing Eve in the foreground booth
through the glass in the act of hanging up. She folds the piece of paper
as she rises and emerges from the booth, her head turned away from us.
Simultaneously, the door of Leonard's booth opens and he steps out.
Without looking at Eve, he crosses over to Vandamm, who is idly
glancing at a magazine at the news-stand. Leonard murmurs something
to him, and the two men move off. Now Eve turns, looks about, and
reacts as she sees:*

### LONG SHOT: POINT OF VIEW
*Thornhill, carrying Eve's small zippered bag, is walking with assumed
nonchalance across the station. He gives a deliberate side glance in Eve's
direction, meaning: 'Follow me.'*

### SEMI-LONG SHOT:
*Eve starts to move across the lobby after Thornhill.*

### CLOSE SHOT: THORNHILL
*He is just coming to a stop at a secluded spot behind a column. He turns
and waits. After a few moments, Eve comes into the shot. She has
assumed a much lighter air. He hands her the zippered bag and several
baggage tickets.*

EVE

What took you so long?

THORNHILL

Small razor. Big face.
> (*glancing about warily*)

Did you get Kaplan?

EVE

Yes.

THORNHILL

Good. What did he say?

EVE

He'll see you, but not at the hotel under any circumstances.
He'll meet you on the outside.

THORNHILL

Where? When?

EVE

I've got it all written out for you.

*She hands him the slip of paper. He studies it as she talks.*

You're to take the Greyhound Bus that leaves Chicago for
Indianapolis at two and ask the driver to let you off at the
Prairie Stop on Highway 41.

THORNHILL
> (*reading*)

Prairie Stop . . . Highway 41 . . .

EVE

About an hour-and-a-half's drive from Chicago.

THORNHILL

I can rent a car.

EVE

No car. Mr Kaplan said bus. He wants to be sure you're
alone.

#### THORNHILL
All right. What do I do when I get there?

#### EVE
Just stand beside the road and wait. He'll be there at three-thirty.

#### THORNHILL
How will I know him?

#### EVE
He'll know *you*. You made the Chicago papers too.

#### THORNHILL
Ah.

#### EVE
Have you got your watch set to Central time?

#### THORNHILL
Yes.
> (*looking at her*)

What's the matter?

#### EVE
Matter?

#### THORNHILL
You. You seem . . . I don't know . . . tense.

#### EVE
> (*turns away*)

You better go. Before the police run out of Redcaps.

#### THORNHILL
We'll see each other again, won't we?

#### EVE
> (*strained*)

Sometime . . . I'm sure . . .

#### THORNHILL
> (*with tenderness*)

I never found a moment to thank you properly.

EVE
(*disturbed*)

Please go.

THORNHILL

But where will I find you?

EVE
(*evasively*)

I have to pick up my bags now . . .

*He takes hold of her, turns her to him.*

THORNHILL

Please wait a minute . . .

*She looks past him.*

EVE

They're coming.

*Thornhill, unable to see over his shoulder because of the column behind him, gives half a glance and dashes off out of the shot. The camera eases over and shoots past Eve's shoulder into the main lobby. There are no police, just a few desultory travellers. Eve turns into the camera and looks after the departed Thornhill with an unhappy expression.*

DISSOLVE TO:

EXT. HIGHWAY 41 – HELICOPTER SHOT – AFTERNOON

*We start close on a Greyhound bus, shooting down on it and travelling along with it as it speeds in an easterly direction at 70 mph. Gradually, camera draws away from the bus, going higher but never losing sight of the vehicle, which recedes into the distance below and becomes a toy-like object on an endless ribbon of deserted highway that stretches across miles of flat prairie. Now the bus is slowing down. It is nearing a junction where a small dirt road coming from nowhere crosses the highway and continues on to nowhere. The bus stops. A man gets out. It is Thornhill. But to us he is only a tiny figure. The bus starts away, moves on out of sight. And now Thornhill stands alone beside the road – a tiny figure in the middle of nowhere.*

*Thornhill glances about, studying his surroundings. The terrain is flat and treeless, even more desolate from this point than it seemed from the air. Here and there patches of low-growing farm crops add some contour to the land. A hot sun beats down. Utter silence hangs heavily in the air. Thornhill glances at his wrist-watch. It is 3:25.*

*In the distance, the faint hum of a motor vehicle is heard. Thornhill looks off to the west. The hum grows louder as the car draws nearer. Thornhill steps closer to the edge of the highway. A black sedan looms up, travelling at high speed. For a moment we are not sure it is not hurtling right at Thornhill. And then it zooms past him, recedes into the distance, becoming a faint hum, a tiny speck, and then silence again.*

*Thornhill takes out a handkerchief, mops his face. He is beginning to sweat now. It could be from nervousness, as well as the heat. Another faint hum, coming from the east, growing louder as he glances off and sees another distant speck becoming a speeding car, this one a closed convertible. Again, anticipation on Thornhill's face. Again, the vague uneasiness of indefinable danger approaching at high speed. And again, zoom – a cloud of dust – a car receding into the distance – a faint hum – and silence.*

*His lips tighten. He glances at his watch again. He steps out into the middle of the highway, looks first in one direction, then the other. Nothing in sight. He loosens his tie, opens his shirt collar, looks up at the sun. Behind him, in the distance, another vehicle is heard approaching. He turns, looks off to the west. This one is a huge transcontinental moving van, roaring towards him at high speed. With quick apprehension he moves off the highway to the dusty side of the road as the van thunders past and disappears. Its fading sound is replaced with a new sound, the chugging of an old flivver.*

*Thornhill looks off in the direction of the approaching sound, sees a flivver nearing the highway from the intersecting dirt road. When the car reaches the highway, it comes to a stop. A middle-aged woman is behind the wheel. Her passenger is a nondescript man of about fifty. He could certainly be a farmer. He gets out of the car. It makes a U-turn and drives off in the direction from which it came. Thornhill watches the man take up a position across the highway from him. The man glances at Thornhill without visible interest, then looks off up the highway towards the east as if waiting for something to come along.*

*Thornhill stares at the man, wondering if this is George Kaplan.*

*The man looks idly across the highway at Thornhill, his face expressionless.*

*Thornhill wipes his face with his handkerchief, never taking his eyes off the man across the highway. The faint sound of an approaching plane has gradually come up over the scene. As the sound grows louder, Thornhill looks up to his left and sees a low-flying biplane approaching from the northwest. He watches it with mounting interest as it heads straight for the spot where he and the stranger face each other across the highway. Suddenly it is upon them, only a hundred feet above the ground, and then, like a giant bird, as Thornhill turns with the plane's passage, it flies over them and continues on.*

*Thornhill stares after the plane, his back to the highway. When the plane has gone several hundred yards beyond the highway, it loses altitude, levels off only a few feet above the ground and begins to fly back and forth in straight lines parallel to the highway, letting loose a trail of powdered dust from beneath its fuselage as it goes. Any farmer would recognize the operation as simple crop-dusting.*

*Thornhill looks across the highway, sees that the stranger is watching the plane with idle interest. Thornhill's lips set with determination. He crosses over and goes up to the Man.*

THORNHILL

Hot day.

MAN

Seen worse.

THORNHILL

Are you . . . uh . . . by any chance supposed to be meeting someone here?

MAN
(still watching the plane)

Waitin' for the bus. Due any minute.

THORNHILL

Oh . . .

MAN

(*idly*)

Some of them crop-duster pilots get rich, if they live long enough . . .

THORNHILL

Then your name isn't . . . Kaplan.

MAN

(*glances at him*)

Can't say it is, 'cause it ain't.

(*he looks off up the highway*)

Well – here she comes, right on time.

*Thornhill looks off to the east, sees a Greyhound bus approaching. The Man peers off at the plane again, and frowns.*

That's funny.

THORNHILL

What?

MAN

That plane's dustin' crops where there ain't no crops.

*Thornhill looks across at the droning plane with growing suspicion as the stranger steps out onto the highway and flags the bus to a stop. Thornhill turns towards the stranger as though to say something to him. But it is too late. The man has boarded the bus, its doors are closing and it is pulling away. Thornhill is alone again.*

*Almost immediately, he hears the plane engine being gunned to a higher speed. He glances off sharply, sees the plane veering off its parallel course and heading towards him. He stands there wide-eyed, rooted to the spot. The plane roars on, a few feet off the ground. There are two men in the twin cockpits, goggled, unrecognizable, menacing. He yells out to them, but his voice is lost in the noise of the plane. In a moment it will be upon him and decapitate him. Desperately he drops to the ground and presses himself flat as the plane zooms over him with a great noise, almost combing his hair with a landing wheel.*

103

*Thornhill scrambles to his feet, sees the plane banking and turning. He looks about wildly, sees a telephone pole and dashes for it as the plane comes at him again. He ducks behind the pole. The plane heads straight for him, veers to the right at the last moment. We hear two sharp cracks of gunfire mixed with the sound of the engine, as two bullets slam into the pole just above Thornhill's head.*

*Thornhill reacts to this new peril, sees the plane banking for another run at him. A car is speeding along the highway from the west. Thornhill dashes out onto the road, tries to flag the car down but the driver ignores him and races by, leaving him exposed and vulnerable as the plane roars in on him. He dives into a ditch and rolls away as another series of shots are heard and bullets rake the ground that he has just occupied.*

*He gets to his feet, looks about, sees a cornfield about fifty yards from the highway, glances up at the plane making its turn, and decides to make a dash for the cover of the tall-growing corn.*

*Shooting down from a helicopter about one hundred feet above the ground, we see Thornhill running towards the cornfield and the plane in pursuit.*

*Shooting from within the cornfield, we see Thornhill come crashing in, scuttling to the right and lying flat and motionless as we hear the plane zoom over him with a burst of gunfire and bullets rip into the corn, but at a safe distance from Thornhill. He raises his head cautiously, gasping for breath, as he hears the plane move off and into its turn.*

*Shooting down from the helicopter, we see the plane levelling off and starting a run over the cornfield, which betrays no sign of the hidden Thornhill. Skimming over the top of the cornstalks, the plane gives forth no burst of gunfire now. Instead, it lets loose thick clouds of poisonous dust which settle down into the corn.*

*Within the cornfield, Thornhill, still lying flat, begins to gasp and choke as the poisonous dust envelops him. Tears stream from his eyes but he does not dare move as he hears the plane coming over the field again. When the plane zooms by and another cloud of dust hits him, he jumps to his feet and crashes out into the open, half blinded and gasping for breath. Far off down the highway to the right, he sees a huge diesel gasoline-tanker approaching. He starts running towards the highway to intercept it.*

Where the plane seems by a mischance to aim at dust in order to get
to his just and makes certain the hero... bewildered and perplexed...
breath. Can or does the frightening air right, he sees a dust-shed?
terrible danger approaching. He starts running towards the farmer's pl-
intercept a

*Shooting from the helicopter, we see Thornhill dashing for the highway, the plane levelling off for another run at him, and the diesel tanker speeding closer.*

*Shooting across the highway, we see Thornhill running and stumbling towards camera, the plane closing in behind him, and the diesel tanker approaching from the left. He dashes out into the middle of the highway and waves his arms wildly.*

*The diesel tanker thunders down the highway towards Thornhill, klaxon blasting impatiently.*

*The plane speeds relentlessly towards Thornhill from the field bordering the highway.*

*Thornhill stands alone and helpless in the middle of the highway, waving his arms. The plane draws closer. The tanker is almost upon him. It isn't going to stop. He can hear the klaxon blasting him out of the way. There is nothing he can do. The plane has caught up with him. The tanker won't stop. It's got to stop. He hurls himself to the pavement directly in its path. There is a scream of brakes and skidding tires, the roar of the plane engine and then a tremendous boom as the diesel truck grinds to a stop inches from Thornhill's body just as the plane, hopelessly committed and caught unprepared by the sudden stop, slams into the travelling gasoline tanker and plane and gasoline explode into a great sheet of flame.*

*In the next few moments, all is confusion. Thornhill, unhurt, rolls out from under the wheels of the diesel truck. The drivers clamber out of the front seat and drop to the highway. Black clouds of smoke billow up from the funeral pyre of the plane and its cremated occupants. We recognize the flaming body of one of the men in the plane. It is Licht, one of Thornhill's original abductors.*

*An elderly open pick-up truck with a second-hand refrigerator standing in it, which has been approaching from the east, pulls up at the side of the road. Its driver, a farmer, jumps out and hurries towards the wreckage.*

FARMER
What happened? What happened?

*The diesel truck drivers are too dazed to answer. Flames and smoke drive them all back. Thornhill, unnoticed, heads towards the unoccupied pick-up truck. Another car comes up from the west, stops, and its driver runs towards the other men. They stare, transfixed, at the holocaust. Suddenly, from behind them, they hear the pick-up truck's motor starting. The farmer who owns the truck turns, and is startled to see his truck being driven away by an utter stranger.*

Hey!

*He runs after the truck. But the stranger – who is Thornhill – steps harder on the accelerator and speeds off in the direction of Chicago.*

DISSOLVE TO:

EXT. MICHIGAN AVENUE, CHICAGO – NIGHT

*The abandoned pick-up truck, with its lonely refrigerator, stands incongruously parked among some new and elegant cars. A patrolman has opened the door and is peering inside.*

EXT. STREET NEAR HOTEL AMBASSADOR EAST

*A police squad car is cruising slowly past the entrances to the Ambassador East and Ambassador West, which face each other on opposite sides of the street. Inside the car, two police lieutenants glance about, eyes searching the area. Camera whips to Thornhill, standing in an attitude of concealment inside the doorway of a darkened store as he watches the police car drive on. He looks quite dishevelled, and his suit would not pass muster at, say, Twenty-One. Now he steps to the sidewalk and starts walking in the direction of the Ambassador East.*

EXT. ENTRANCE HOTEL AMBASSADOR EAST

*Thornhill approaches the hotel and enters.*

INT. LOBBY HOTEL AMBASSADOR EAST

*Thornhill crosses the lobby to the desk and waits for a Clerk to come over.*

CLERK
(*eyeing him with distaste*)
Yes?

THORNHILL

Could you let me have Mr George Kaplan's room number, please?

CLERK

(*thoughtfully*)

Kaplan . . .

(*as he starts to one side to consult files*)

I think he checked out . . .

THORNHILL

Checked out?

CLERK

(*returns with a file card*)

That's right. Checked out at seven-ten this morning.

THORNHILL

Seven-ten? Are you sure?

CLERK

Yes. Left a forwarding address – Hotel Sheraton-Johnson, Rapid City, South Dakota.

*Thornhill has taken out the slip of paper on which Eve had given him directions to meet Kaplan.*

THORNHILL

(*talking half to himself*)

Seven-ten? Then how come I got a message from him at nine-thir–?

CLERK

What was that?

THORNHILL

Nothing, nothing.

*His eyes narrow and his jaw tightens with realization. He crumples the piece of paper into a ball and hurls it away in anger. Just then he looks up and sees Eve, who has come through the entrance to the lobby. She does not see him as she goes directly to the news-stand and buys an evening paper. Thornhill draws back, watches her unobserved as she glances quickly at the front page while hurrying to a waiting elevator. She steps in, the door closes and the elevator starts up. Thornhill watches the floor indicator until the elevator stops. Then he turns back to the Clerk.*

THORNHILL

Sorry to bother you again.

CLERK

Uh-huh.

THORNHILL

Miss Eve Kendall is expecting me. Room four-something-or-other. I've forgotten the number. Would you mind?

*The Clerk steps to one side, examines his listings, then returns to Thornhill.*

CLERK

She's in four sixty-three.

THORNHILL

Thanks.

*He hurries towards the elevator as the Clerk looks after him.*

QUICK DISSOLVE TO:

HOTEL CORRIDOR. FOURTH FLOOR

*Thornhill approaches the door to 463, looks up and down the corridor if for no other reason than to indicate to us that he has now become suspicious, cautious and surreptitious in matters pertaining to Eve. He puts an ear to her door, listens, hears nothing. He presses the buzzer and waits. Presently the door opens and she sees him standing before her. Her eyes widen. She is too stunned to say anything.*

THORNHILL
(*pleasantly*)

Hello.

*He goes right past her into the room.*

INT. EVE'S HOTEL ROOM

*Eve turns, stares at Thornhill as she closes the door behind him. If his back were not to her, he would see the mixed emotions on her face – not just surprise, but overwhelming relief, too. But relief is not something she can afford to reveal too strongly, because that would indicate that there was something to be relieved about. She is almost completely controlled by the time Thornhill turns to her, after a very brief moment in which his darting glance has taken in the room, and the open door to the bathroom, and noticed nothing worthy of apprehension.*

THORNHILL

Surprised?

EVE

Yes.

*She stares at him, still shaken.*

THORNHILL

No getting rid of *me*, is there?

*Suddenly Eve goes up to him, puts her arms around him, holds him close and presses her face to his breast. Is it tenderness and relief, or merely the need to hide from the double-edged meaning of his last remark? Thornhill puts his hands on her, but without affection. He knows he is on to something now, and he intends to play it cool. Occasionally his deep down anger will make him say incautious things he oughtn't to say if he intends to disarm the girl – and just as occasionally, he will be even warmer than he intended to be. He can't help liking this female a little bit, even while he would like to slug her. It's because he remembers last night. It's because, also, she happens to be of the opposite sex.*

I need a drink.

EVE

I have some scotch.

THORNHILL

With water. No ice.

*Eve disengages herself from him and goes over to a table where drinking things are set up. Thornhill takes the opportunity to saunter over to a chair where the newspaper has been thrown. The front-page story is plainly visible:*

## TWO DIE AS CROP-DUSTER PLANE CRASHES
### Low-flying craft hits oil tanker.
### Truck drivers escape holocaust.

*During this, and while Eve is mixing drinks, they are talking:*

EVE
*(too casually)*

How did it go today?

THORNHILL

The meeting with Kaplan?

EVE

Uh-huh.

THORNHILL
*(just as casually)*

He didn't show up.

EVE

Oh?

THORNHILL
*(staring at her back)*

Funny, isn't it?

EVE
*(after a slight pause)*

Why funny?

THORNHILL

After all those very involved and very explicit directions he
gave you on the phone.

EVE

Maybe I copied them down wrong.

THORNHILL

I don't think you got them wrong. I think you sent me to the
right place all right.

*He couldn't resist that one. Fortunately for Eve, her face is not turned to
him, and she can always fumble with glasses and stirring rods.*

III

**EVE**

Why not call him again and see what happened?

**THORNHILL**

I did. He checked out, went to South Dakota.

**EVE**

South Dakota?

**THORNHILL**

Rapid City.

**EVE**
(*after a moment*)

What are you going to do next?

**THORNHILL**

I haven't made up my mind yet. It may depend on you.

*On this, Eve turns, with the drinks in her hands.*

**EVE**

On me?

*She walks up to him.*

**THORNHILL**

You're my little helper, aren't you?

*He takes a glass from her, all the while staring into her eyes.*

To us.
(*he touches his glass to hers*)
To a long and lasting friendship . . .
(*he takes a sip*)
Meaning, from now on, I'm not going to let *you* out of my sight, sweetheart.

**EVE**
(*hiding in her glass*)

I'm afraid you're going to have to, Thornhill.

**THORNHILL**
(*shakes his head*)

Unh-uh.

112

(*turning away*)

I do have plans of my own, you know – and you do have
problems.

*Thornhill takes a long drag on his drink before he speaks, and once
again he engraves each word on a Gillette Blue Blade.*

**THORNHILL**

Wouldn't it be nice if my problems and your plans were
somehow . . . *connected*?
   (*her quick glance finds his face smiling softly, nay lovingly*)
Then we could stay close to each other from here on in and
not have to go off in separate directions. Togetherness. Know
what I mean?

*Eve stares at him for a moment saying nothing, and is saved by the bell
as the phone rings. She glances at it, but makes no move to answer it.*

Go ahead. It can't be for *me*.

*She hesitates uncertainly. The phone rings again. He makes a move as
though he will answer it. Quickly Eve walks over to the night-table
between the beds and picks up the phone, while Thornhill saunters
around the room just as though he were not utterly alert and keenly
interested in every monosyllable of her tightly-controlled conversation.*

**EVE**
(*to phone*)

Hello?
         (*listens*)
Yes.
         (*listens*)
No, don't. I'm not dressed yet.
         (*listens*)
What time?
         (*listens*)
I'll meet you.
         (*listens*)
What's the address?

*She takes up a pencil, writes something down on a memo pad as she listens. Thornhill observes this out of the corner of his glance.*

All right.

(*listens*)

I will.

(*listens*)

Goodbye.

*She hangs up, tears off the page on which she has written something, walks over to her handbag on the dresser and puts the slip of paper inside. We see a gun in her handbag.*

THORNHILL

Business?

EVE

Yes.

THORNHILL

Industrial designing business?

EVE

Mm hmmm.

*He goes up behind her, puts his hands about her waist. (The nice thing about this kind of cat-and-mouse work is that you can enjoy yourself while you're doing it, because it's part of the game.) Eve is disturbed by the nearness of him, and his hands on her.*

THORNHILL

All work and no play. Girl like you should be enjoying herself tonight instead of taking phone calls from clients. How about dinner with *me* just for openers?

EVE

You can't afford to be seen anywhere.

THORNHILL

What's wrong with up here? Our own little Pump Room for two.

*Eve pulls out of his grasp, moves away from him.*

EVE

No . . . I . . . I can't.

114

**THORNHILL**
*(easily)*

I insist.

*Eve is in a spot. She gets control of herself before she turns to him. But a little desperation does creep through in her voice.*

**EVE**

I want you to do me a favor, Thornhill – a big, big favor.

**THORNHILL**

Name it.

**EVE**

I want you to leave, right now. Stay far away from me and don't come near me again. We're *not* going to get involved. Last night was last night and that's all there was, that's all there is, there isn't going to be anything more between us. So please – goodbye, good luck, no conversation. Just leave.

**THORNHILL**
*(utterly unperturbed)*

Right away?

**EVE**

Yes.

**THORNHILL**

No questions asked?

**EVE**

Yes.

*Thornhill looks at her a moment. She wants to get rid of him. She's got to get rid of him. That's for sure. He shakes his head.*

**THORNHILL**

Unh-uh.

**EVE**

Please . . .

**THORNHILL**

After dinner.

Now.

                    THORNHILL
                    (*firmly*)
After dinner. Fair is fair.

*Eve's lips tighten, but she is careful not to betray the urgency of her
situation. The wheels go round for a moment as she looks at him. Then,
she makes a decision, softens her expression, and smiles.*

                    EVE
All right. On one condition.
          (*she goes up to him, touches his rumpled, dirty suit*)
You've got to let the hotel valet do something with that suit
first. You belong in the *stockyards* looking like that.

                    THORNHILL
                    (*shrugs*)
I'm very large with pigs this year.

                    EVE
                    (*pointing*)
There's the phone.

*She turns to the mirror and starts to fix her hair. Thornhill goes over to
the bed, sits down and puts his hand on the phone but doesn't pick it up.
He is thinking fast. With a cautious glance over his shoulder, he slides
his hand to the memo pad beside the phone and tilts it slightly. He sees
something there on the pad but we do not see what it is. Now he picks
up the phone.*

                    THORNHILL
                    (*to phone*)
Valet service, please . . . Valet? This is . . . uh . . .
          (*to Eve*)
Where are we?

                    EVE
Four sixty-three.

THORNHILL
(to phone)
This is room four sixty-three. How long would it take to get a
suit sponged and pressed real fast? . . . Twenty minutes? Fine
. . . Four sixty-three.
(he hangs up)
He'll be right up.

EVE
Better take your things off.

THORNHILL
(going up to her)
What am I going to do with my clothes off for twenty
minutes?
(an afterthought, as he gazes at her reflection in the mirror)
Couldn't he take an *hour*?

EVE
(turns, practically in his arms)
You could always take a cold shower.

*She starts to help him off with his jacket as he takes his things out of his
pockets and places them on the dresser. Both of them are playing it just
as though they were up to nothing but good, clean, healthy love-play.*

THORNHILL
When I was a little boy, I never even let my *mother* undress
me.

EVE
(peeling off the jacket)
Well, you're a big boy now.

*She tosses the jacket on the bed, turns back to him, puts her hands on
his belt buckle, starts to unfasten it. He takes her hands in his.*

THORNHILL
How did a girl like you ever get to be a girl like you?

EVE
Lucky, I guess.

117

Not lucky – wicked . . . naughty . . . up to no good . . . Ever kill anyone?

*Instantly Eve's expression changes. He has gone dangerously too far; quickly he takes the curse off the remark.*

Bet you could tease a man to death without even trying.
>                     (*he pats her cheek*)

So stop trying, hm?

*He starts towards the bathroom, undoing the belt buckle himself as he goes. The door buzzer sounds. Eve goes to the door, opens it, lets the valet in.*

>                     EVE
>                 (*to the valet*)

Be right with you.
>                 (*she goes to the half open bathroom door*)

Trousers, please.

*Thornhill's hand comes out with the trousers. Eve takes them, picks up the jacket on the bed, gives the suit to the valet and closes the door behind him. From the bathroom she hears Thornhill's voice calling out to her:*

>                 THORNHILL'S VOICE

Think I'll take that cold shower after all.

>                     EVE

Good.

*Next she hears the shower being turned on, then Thornhill's voice raised in a loud, shower-stall rendition of 'The Night They Invented Champagne'. Immediately, and with urgent haste, Eve prepares to leave. She goes to the closet, gets the jacket of her suit, puts it on. Then from a dresser drawer she takes some papers and stuffs them into her handbag, darting occasional glances towards the partially open bathroom door from whence comes Thornhill's 'Singin' in the Rain'.*

*Her glance falls on Thornhill's belongings, which he had removed from his pockets. A closer view of them shows the torn newspaper photograph of Vandamm covered by Thornhill's 'ROT' initialled matchbook. Eve's hand sets the matches aside, picks up the torn newspaper photograph, holds it long enough for quick study and puts it down again. In a wider angle she turns, and, with a final glance around, starts out of the room.*

INT. BATHROOM

*Thornhill is not in the shower after all. In shirt, tie, shorts, socks and shoes, he has been standing at the crack in the door peering out at Eve's furtive activities while singing lustily, the shower spraying away busily behind him. Now he hears the outer door close as Eve makes her hasty exit.*

CLOSE SHOT: THORNHILL

*As he opens the bathroom door wider, steps out into the room. It is clear from his expression that he has not really been duped, but rather has been ahead of this little game all along. He goes to the night-table, picks up the memo pad on which Eve had made a notation and removed the top sheet. He picks up a pencil and in a closer angle we see him trace in the indentation left by Eve's pencil. It reads:* 'I212 N. MICHIGAN'.

DISSOLVE TO:

EXT. MICHIGAN AVE., CHICAGO — NIGHT

*A taxi pulls up and Thornhill steps out. (His suit is in fine shape now.) He glances about, sees that he has the right address, and moves across the sidewalk.*

CLOSER ANGLE — EXT. SHAW & OPPENHEIM GALLERIES

*The lighted window of a rather elegant art gallery. A sign in the window announces:*

'AUCTION TONIGHT — 8:00 P.M.
FURNITURE AND OBJETS D'ART FROM
THE COLLECTION OF DR ORLANDO MENDOZA'

*Over the door, the building number:* 'I212'. *Thornhill frowns, puzzled, takes out the slip of paper, looks up at the number again, then decides to go inside.*

AUCTIONEER

Thank you, sir. Four hundred fifty dollars is bid for the pair, can I hear five hundred, will you say five hundred, can I say the five hundred, fair warning and last call – sold to Mr Stone second row.

*On the stage the chairs are removed as lot 103, an Aubusson settee is brought onto the stage.*

CLOSE SHOT: *Vandamm's fingers gently moving over the soft flesh of Eve's neck. Camera draws back to include Eve seated, Vandamm standing behind her and Leonard beyond them seated on a low table, his legs dangling. At the far end of the room is a raised platform on which an Auctioneer and his Assistant, with the aid of portable microphones, are going about the business of unloading various objets d'art. Elderly men in black dust-jackets pass the items from the wings on to the stage, one piece at a time, where each object is then auctioned off at the leisurely pace which distinguishes the sale of nineteenth-century French paintings from the sale of twentieth-century American tobacco. Most of the hundred-odd spectators at the auction are seated on folding chairs in the center of the room. Moving along the aisle on either side of them are several handsome young women employed by the gallery to jot down the names of successful bidders, should they not be known. Beyond these aisles, on either side, is the overflow of spectators, some of them seated, some standing, others leaning against antique period furniture.*

Lot number 103. Ah! this lovely Aubusson settee, in excellent condition, please start the bidding. How much? Eight hundred dollars is offered, thank you. Eight hundred is bid, say the nine, go nine hundred. Nine hundred is bid, now who'll say one thousand? One thousand, thank you, one thousand, at one thousand, say eleven hundred, bid the eleven hundred, not enough for this choice piece, can I hear eleven hundred? Selling at one thousand, once at one thousand, twice, last call. Do I hear eleven hundred? Sold! One thousand to Mrs Sheridan.

*The settee is removed from the stage and lot 104, a barometer, is brought in.*

Lot number 104 – This eighteenth-century hand-carved barometer. Can I say two hundred and fifty to start? That gentleman says one hundred and fifty. I have one hundred and fifty. Say two hundred, two hundred is bid here, now go the three

*Camera reaches the end of the dolly and pans to Thornhill, standing in entrance, staring off at Vandamm and the others. Thornhill's mouth tightens with anger. It is not that he is overwhelmed with surprise at this visible evidence of alliance, but it does remove any lingering doubts he might still have had about the girl. He has really been taken for a ride – almost, but not quite, all the way. And now, those fingers playing at the back of her neck. The hell with caution, and concealing anger. Besides, it's too late. He moves out of shot.*

*Thornhill moves to a chair near the group.*

THORNHILL
The three of you together. Now there's a picture only Charles Addams could draw.

VANDAMM
(*unperturbed*)
Good evening, Mr Kaplan –

THORNHILL
(*bitterly*)
Before we start calling each other names, maybe you better tell me yours. I haven't had the pleasure.

VANDAMM
– You disappoint me, sir . . .

hundred, say three hundred, three hundred is bid, thank you. Do I hear three hundred and fifty? Three hundred and fifty, may I have three hundred and fifty, three hundred, three hundred twice, third and last call. Do I hear three hundred and fifty? Sold! Mr Echart three hundred.

*The barometer is removed and lot 105 is brought in.*

**THORNHILL**
(*bitterly at Eve*)
I was just going to say that to *her*.

*Eve stares straight ahead. Vandamm gazes off at the Auctioneer.*

**VANDAMM**
I've always understood you to be a pretty shrewd fellow at your job. What possessed you to come blundering in here like this? Could it be an overpowering interest in art?

**THORNHILL**
Yes. The art of survival.
(*a quick shaft at Leonard*)
Poured any good drunks lately?

**EVE**
(*in a hollow voice, to Vandamm*)
He followed me here from
the hotel.

**LEONARD**
(*to Eve*)
He was in your room?

*She nods. Vandamm reacts with
displeasure.*

**THORNHILL**
(*with contempt*)
Sure. Isn't everybody?

Now, ladies and gentlemen –
number 105, an excellent
example of pre-Columbian
art. It dates from about
1000 AD. A Tarascan warrior
from the State of Kolemia, in
Mexico. May I hear a starting
bid worthy of this fine art
piece? Who will say one
thousand dollars to start?
The gentleman here suggests
five hundred. All right, that's
a start. Now say one
thousand. I have five
hundred dollars, may I say
the thousand? Seven
hundred and fifty is offered.
Thank you, now say the
thousand. One thousand is
bid, make it twelve hundred
and fifty. Eleven hundred,
you say? All right I have
eleven hundred bid, make it
twelve hundred – twelve
hundred dollars there. Now

*At this time, the Auctioneer's
voice is heard announcing item
number 105. He proceeds to
describe it. During this, an
attendant has been walking about
showing the figure to the
spectators. Leonard taps the
momentarily distracted Vandamm
on the shoulder and points to the
figure. Vandamm glances at it
quickly, looks up at Leonard and
says:*

**VANDAMM**
Yes.

**THORNHILL**
(*to Vandamm*)
I didn't realize you were an
art collector. I thought you
just collected corpses.

*The bidding has started.*

**VANDAMM**
(*to Leonard, quietly*)
Fifteen hundred.

thirteen is here, fourteen
hundred is bid.
    (*off-screen*)
Fifteen hundred I'm bid,
who'll say seventeen fifty –
do I hear seventeen fifty?

Seventeen fifty is bid. Say
two thousand – two thousand
anyone – do I hear two
thousand? Seventeen fifty is
bid. Seventeen fifty, are you
all through at seventeen fifty?
Sold then to Mr Vandamm
at seventeen fifty.

*The Tarascan piece is removed
and lot 106, a Louis XV curio
cabinet is brought in.*

Number 106 – for your
pleasure is this Louis XV
curio cabinet of gold and
bronze doré with Vernis
Martin figured decorations
and landscape painting. Who
will say five hundred dollars

*Leonard makes a silent signal to
the auctioneer.*

THORNHILL
(*looking down at Eve*)
I'll bet you paid plenty for
this little piece of –
sculpture –

VANDAMM
(*to Leonard*)
Seventeen fifty.

*Eve is visibly suffering.*

THORNHILL
(*continuing*)
She's worth every dollar, take
it from me. She really puts
her heart into her work. In
fact her whole body.
    (*a quick glance at Leonard*)
And where does he keep *you*
– in a curio cabinet?

*Thornhill reacts to the
Auctioneer's mention of
Vandamm's name.*

    (*hearing the name*)
Vandamm, huh?

VANDAMM
(*turns to Thornhill*)
Has anyone ever told you
that you overplay your
various roles rather severely,
Mr Kaplan? First you're the
outraged Madison Avenue
man who claims he has been
mistaken for someone else.

to start the bidding? Five hundred dollars for it. Five hundred dollars for it. All right I'll accept your start of two hundred dollars, two hundred is bid, go three, two fifty I have, say three, two fifty I have, say three hundred, three hundred now go four, three go four, three go four, three go four, three go four, three twenty-five is bid, say fifty, three fifty I have, say four, three hundred and fifty, go four hundred, three hundred and fifty, say three seventy-five, three hundred fifty, say seventy-five. Don't lose it for twenty-five dollars; thank you three hundred and seventy-five is bid. I have three hundred and seventy-five dollars, go the four hundred. Three seventy-five, go four. Four hundred dollars is bid. Say four hundred and twenty-five. Four hundred twenty-five once, four hundred twenty-five twice, last call at four hundred twenty-five. Sold to the lady in the fourth row for four hundred dollars.

*The Louis XV cabinet is removed and lot 107 is brought in.*

And now, ladies and gentlemen, we offer Catalogue number 107 – this

Then you play a fugitive from justice, supposedly trying to clear his name of a crime he knows he didn't commit. And now, you play the peevish lover, stung by jealousy and betrayal.
(*a chilly smile*)
Seems to me you fellows could stand a little less training from the FBI and a little more from the Actors' Studio.

THORNHILL
Apparently the only performance that's going to satisfy *you* is when I play dead.

VANDAMM
(*gently*)
Your very next role. You will be quite convincing, I assure you.

*Leonard has already started out of the room to arrange that.*

THORNHILL
(*watching him go*)
I wonder what subtle form of manslaughter is next on the program. Am I going to be dropped into a vat of molten steel and become part of some new skyscraper?
(*looking at Eve*)
Or are you going to ask *this* . . . female to kiss me again and *poison* me to death?

rare Marcolini Meissen compote, acquired by Dr Mendoza from the estate of the Comtesse de Chivre. How much to start the bidding on this collector's porcelain? Five hundred, madam? That's an extremely low start and should prompt spirited bidding. Six? Six hundred I have, now the seven, seven hundred I have, thank you, say eight. May I direct your attention to the magnificent *répoussé* flowers on this outstanding example. Eight hundred dollars there, nine hundred in the front. One thousand is bid on the far side. Eleven hundred dollars is here now, say the twelve, twelve hundred dollars there. Twelve hundred is bid, say thirteen hundred, may I hear thirteen hundred please? Fair selling at twelve hundred. Do I hear thirteen hundred? Last call, sold twelve hundred dollars. Thank you.

*The Marcolini Meissen compote is removed and lot 108, the Vienna plates, is displayed.*

Number 108 – we offer you now twelve Royal Vienna

*Eve gets to her feet, turns and slaps him in the face. He grabs her wrists and they stare at each other for a moment.*

(*with contempt*)
Who are you kidding? You *have* no feelings to hurt.

*He firmly presses her back down into her seat. During this, a man in the audience nearby is half turned, as though he has been observing the entire altercation.* It is the Professor of the CIA.

VANDAMM
(*angrily*)
Mr Kaplan –

THORNHILL
(*turning on him*)
Look, Vandamm, I don't know why you want me dead, but this I –

VANDAMM
(*interrupting*)
– We've had just about enough of you . . .

THORNHILL
Then why don't you call the police? No – that's the last thing you want – me in the hands of the police. There's something I might tell them, huh? That's why you had this one here hustle me on the train last night, like the good little industrial designer that she is. Well, something tells

plates, magnificently hand-decorated with portraits of Court beauties. How much a piece and take the lot? Thirty a piece is bid all over the house. Thirty-five, say forty, forty go forty-five, forty-five I have, go fifty – fifty go five, fifty go five, fifty is here, say fifty-five, fifty dollars a piece, say fifty-five, anymore, sir? Sold then for fifty dollars a piece.

*The plates are taken out as a painting is brought in.*

Catalogue number 109. A superb example of this early nineteenth-century master. It will enhance any collection of fine art. What is your pleasure? How much to start? One thousand is bid, twelve-fifty I have, fifteen hundred, fifteen hundred is bid, say seventeen fifty, I have seventeen fifty, two thousand is bid –

me I've got a much better chance of survival if I *go* to the police. And the mere fact that you don't *want* me to is enough for me.

(*to Eve*)
Goodnight, sweetheart. Don't think it hasn't been nice.

*He walks away from them and goes towards the entrance in the rear. But he doesn't get very far before he stops. Standing inside the doorway waiting for him is Valerian, the UN assassin. Thornhill turns, looks about, and sees down the aisle, the steps to the Auctioneer's stage where men are bringing on a piece of furniture for auction. He starts down the aisle with the intention of making his way out through the back. Then he slows down as he sees Leonard stepping out of the 'wings' of the stage. Leonard looks at him steadily, and then withdraws significantly. Thornhill looks about him with desperation, then quickly slips into a nearby seat among the spectators. At this moment, Vandamm and Eve depart. Thornhill turns his attention to the platform, where the Auctioneer has a painting on the block.*

(NOTE: Pick up dialogue in script.)

**AUCTIONEER**

I have two thousand. Do I hear twenty-five? . . . Twenty-five
hundred please . . . Twenty-two fifty. Thank you. Do I hear
twenty-five? . . . Twenty-two fifty once. Twenty-two fifty
twice. Last call . . .

**THORNHILL**
(*shouts*)

Fifteen hundred!

**AUCTIONEER**
(*startled*)

The bid is already up to twenty-two fifty, sir.

**THORNHILL**

I *still* say fifteen hundred!

*Heads turn towards him angrily. But Thornhill is concerned only about
escaping the fate Valerian and Leonard have reserved for him.*

**AUCTIONEER**
(*recovering*)

I have twenty-two fifty. Do I hear twenty-five hundred? . . .
Twenty-two fifty once. Twenty-two fifty twice . . .

**THORNHILL**

Twelve hundred!

**AUCTIONEER**
(*quickly*)

Sold for twenty-two fifty. And now –

**THORNHILL**
(*loudly*)

Twenty-two fifty for *that chromo*?

**AUCTIONEER**
(*ignoring him*)

– Number 116 in the catalogue . . .
(*as attendants bring out a chaise longue*)
'A Louis XIV carved and painted *lit de repos.*' Kindly observe
the moulded frame, the carved, freestanding columns at each

corner and the fluted, tapering legs. Will somebody start the bidding at seven hundred and fifty dollars, please?

#### THORNHILL

How do we know it's not a fake? It *looks* like a fake!

*An elderly Woman seated directly in front of Thornhill turns and glares at him.*

#### WOMAN

One thing we know: *you're* no fake. You're a *genuine* idiot.

#### THORNHILL

Thank you.

#### AUCTIONEER

I wonder if I could respectfully ask the gentleman to get into the spirit of the proceedings here.

#### THORNHILL

All right. I'll start it at eight.

#### AUCTIONEER

Eight hundred dollars. Thank you. Nine hundred . . . One thousand I have. Go twelve.

#### THORNHILL

Eleven!

#### AUCTIONEER

Eleven is bid. Go twelve. Who'll say twelve? Eleven once. Who'll say twelve? Eleven twice. Twelve. Thank you. Twelve is bid. I have twelve. Go thirteen. Who'll say thirteen?

#### THORNHILL

Thirteen dollars!

#### AUCTIONEER

You mean thirteen hundred, sir?

#### THORNHILL

I mean thirteen *dollars*, which is more than it's worth!

*The Auctioneer will continue his work, but his assistant will now reach for the phone on his desk and make a hurried call, which will not go unnoticed by Thornhill.*

**AUCTIONEER**

Twelve hundred I have. Go thirteen. Who'll say thirteen?
Twelve fifty? Twelve hundred once. Twelve hundred twice.
Last call. Twelve hundred.

**THORNHILL**

Two thousand!

**AUCTIONEER**
(*a little stunned*)

Two thousand?

**THORNHILL**

Twenty-one hundred!

**AUCTIONEER**

I'm sorry, sir, but we can't –

**THORNHILL**

Make it twenty-five hundred!

*By this time an angry murmur is rising from the spectators. Someone
shouts: 'Ask him to leave!' A uniformed male Attendant is moving
down the aisle towards Thornhill. Valerian and Leonard, in their
separate positions, are glancing about uncertainly.*

**AUCTIONEER**

Would the gentleman *please* cooperate?

**ASSISTANT AUCTIONEER**
(*trying to restore order*)

The last bid was twelve hundred.

**THORNHILL**

Twenty-five hundred! My money is as good as anybody's!

**AUCTIONEER**

I have twelve hundred once . . . twelve hundred twice . . .

**THORNHILL**

Three thousand!

**AUCTIONEER**

Last call. Sold for twelve hundred.

THORNHILL
*(leaping to his feet)*
You're not going to get away with this!

*By this time the uniformed Attendant has reached Thornhill's row of seats, pushed into the row and grabbed him by the arm.*

Let go of me! Get your hands off me or I'll sue!

*Now the place is really in an uproar. Spectators push Thornhill into the aisle. He grapples with the Attendant as women cry out in alarm. Two Police Officers come running in through the entrance. Thornhill notices this with a pleased expression, hauls back and lets the Attendant have a good one on the jaw. The man goes reeling back into the crowd, bounces back and lets fly a swing at Thornhill, who ducks, moves in and wrestles him to the floor. During this, just after the police arrive, the Professor gets up and quickly walks out. The police now reach the struggle, seize Thornhill and pull him to his feet.*

FIRST OFFICER
All right now . . .

THORNHILL
What took you so long?

SECOND OFFICER
*(pulling him towards the door)*
Let's take a little walk . . .

THORNHILL
Wait a minute . . .

SECOND OFFICER
Get moving.

THORNHILL
I haven't finished bidding yet . . .

FIRST OFFICER
*(dragging him along)*
Yeah, yeah.

> THORNHILL
> (*struggling*)
> Three thousand! It's mine for three thousand!

*Nearing the entrance they approach Valerian, standing there completely frustrated. Thornhill flashes him an apologetic smile as he is dragged by.*

> Sorry, old man. But keep trying.

*Valerian watches without expression as Thornhill is escorted safely past him.*

ANOTHER ANGLE
*Thornhill and the two policemen continue through the lobby. Behind them is a telephone booth. We see the Professor standing beside it watching Thornhill being taken out. After they have passed him, the Professor glances after them briefly, then goes into the booth and closes the door.*

EXT. SHAW & OPPENHEIM GALLERIES

*The police emerge from the building with Thornhill and hurry him towards a patrol car parked at the curb.*

> THORNHILL
> Handle with care, fellahs . . .

> FIRST OFFICER
> (*opening rear door*)
> In there.

> THORNHILL
> . . . I'm valuable property.

> FIRST OFFICER
> In.

*He pushes Thornhill into the car.*

INT. PATROL CAR

*Thornhill lands on the rear seat and the first officer joins him, while the other cop gets behind the wheel.*

**THORNHILL**

I want to thank you boys for saving my life –

**FIRST OFFICER**
(*gruffly*)

Save it for the station-house.

*The car starts away.*

**THORNHILL**
(*buoyantly*)

Come on. Let's see some smiles and good cheer. You're about to become heroes. Know who I am?

**FIRST OFFICER**
(*disinterested*)

We'll find out as soon as we book ya for bein' drunk and disorderly.

**THORNHILL**

Drunk and disorderly? That's chicken feed. You've hit the *jackpot*, Sergeant . . .
(*as the Sergeant gives him a bored look*)
'Chicago police capture United Nations slayer.'

*Now the look is not so bored. Thornhill hands the half-believing sergeant his wallet saying:*

Roger Thornhill is the name. Take me to your leader.

*While the Sergeant is quickly looking over Thornhill's identification cards, the Officer behind the wheel picks up a newspaper, glances at it, turns back to look at Thornhill and holds up the paper.*

**SECOND OFFICER**

It's him!

*In the back seat, the Sergeant leans forward, stares off-screen at the paper, then turns and looks at Thornhill.*

**THORNHILL**

Congratulations, men.

(*awed*)

Yeah . . .

*The man behind the wheel has taken up the telephone receiver on the dashboard and put in a call to headquarters. (The phone is similar to household instruments. We can hear only one end of the conversation.) During this, Thornhill sits back with smug expression.*

SECOND OFFICER
(*to phone*)

This is one-oh-five-five. Sergeant Flamm. We got a man here answering to the description of Thornhill, Roger. Code seventy-six. Wanted by NYPD. Positive ID.

(*listens*)

Absolutely. No question.

(*listens*)

Michigan Avenue. Proceeding west to forty-second precinct.

(*listens*)

What?

(*listens*)

Come again?

(*listens*)

Ya sure?

(*listens*)

Okay.

(*listens*)

Right.

(*listens*)

Yeah. I got it.

(*listens*)

One-oh-five-five off and clear.

*He hangs up, makes a swift U-turn and speeds off in the opposite direction.*

FIRST OFFICER
(*startled*)

Where we goin'?

134

> SECOND OFFICER
> *(dejected)*

The airport.

> FIRST OFFICER

For what?

> SECOND OFFICER
> *(disgusted)*

Orders.

> THORNHILL

Just a second here. I'm not going to any airport. I want to be taken to police headquarters.

> SECOND OFFICER

Ya *do*, huh?

> THORNHILL
> *(leans forward)*

Why do you think I *sent* for you fellows?

> SECOND OFFICER

How *about* this guy, Charley? He sent for us.

> FIRST OFFICER
> *(pulling Thornhill back)*

Sit back.

> THORNHILL

Did you hear what I said? I want to be taken to police headquarters! I'm a dangerous assassin! I'm a mad killer on the loose!

> SECOND OFFICER

You oughta be ashamed of yourself.

DISSOLVE TO:

EXT. MIDWAY AIRPORT, CHICAGO – NIGHT

*The police car pulls up, stops. The two Police Officers get out. Thornhill gets out. They walk him into the terminal. In the background, the sound of planes taking off.*

135

*They enter, and the police escort Thornhill to the Information Counter.*

**SECOND OFFICER**

They said right here.

**THORNHILL**
(*grumbling*)

Does anybody mind if I sit down? I've been running all day.

*Just then, the police see a man rushing through the door towards them. It is the Professor. He is breathless as he goes up to the Information Desk, giving Thornhill and the police a quick glance as he goes. We see the Professor lean over the desk and murmur something to the clerk, who nods, acknowledges him and immediately hands him an envelope of plane tickets. The clerk leans over his desk and points down the terminal building. The Professor turns and approaches the group, still out of breath. The camera moves into a closer angle. The Professor fumbles in his pockets, brings out an identification, which he shows to the police, all the while saying:*

**PROFESSOR**

Never thought I'd make it. Getting too old for this kind of work.
(*he glances at Thornhill*)
All right. Thank you, men.
(*takes Thornhill by the arm*)
Let's go, Mr Thornhill. We haven't much time. This way is more private.

*The following scene will be played in a fast-moving dolly shot as the Professor escorts Thornhill away from the police through the terminal, along a ramp, through a gate and across the field towards a waiting passenger plane. Movement will come to a halt only where indicated.*

**THORNHILL**

I don't think I caught your name.

**PROFESSOR**

I don't think I pitched it.

You're police, aren't you? Or is it FBI?

FBI . . . CIA . . . ONI . . . we're all in the same alphabet
soup.

Well, put this in your alphabet soup: I had nothing to do with
that United Nations killing . . .

We know that.

(*slows down*)
You do?

(*bumping a passerby*)
Sorry.

Then what's the idea of the police chasing *me* all over the
map?

We never interfere with the police unless absolutely
necessary. It has become necessary.

I take it, then, I'm to be cleared.

(*taking his arm*)
I do wish you'd walk faster, Mr Thornhill. We'll miss the
plane.

(*walking faster*)
Where are we going – New York or Washington?

Rapid City, South Dakota.

THORNHILL
(*suspicious*)

Rapid City? What for?

PROFESSOR

It's near Mt Rushmore.

THORNHILL

I've already seen Mt Rushmore.

PROFESSOR

So has your friend Mr Vandamm.

THORNHILL
(*slowing down again*)

Vandamm?

PROFESSOR
(*wrily*)

A rather formidable gentleman, eh?

THORNHILL
(*with venom*)

And what about that treacherous tramp with him . . .

PROFESSOR

Miss Kendall?

THORNHILL

Yeah.

PROFESSOR

His mistress. We know all about her.

THORNHILL
(*bridling at this*)

What's Vandamm up to?

PROFESSOR
(*evasively*)

Let's say he's a kind of . . . importer-exporter.

THORNHILL

Of what?

PROFESSOR

Oh . . . you could say . . . government secrets perhaps?

THORNHILL

Why don't you grab him?

PROFESSOR

Too much we still don't know about his organization.

THORNHILL

Uh-huh. Well what's Mt Rushmore got to do with all this?

PROFESSOR

Vandamm has a place near there. We think it's his jumping-off point to leave the country tomorrow night.

THORNHILL

And you're going to stop him . . .

PROFESSOR

No.

THORNHILL
(puzzled)

Then . . . what are we *going* there for?

PROFESSOR

To set his mind at ease about George Kaplan.

*Thornhill glances sharply at the Professor and peers at him for a moment.*

THORNHILL

You, huh?

PROFESSOR

Eh?

THORNHILL
(a statement)

You're George Kaplan, *aren't* you . . .

PROFESSOR
(blandly)

Oh no, Mr Thornhill. There *is* no such person as George Kaplan.

*Thornhill comes to a dead stop.*

THORNHILL

*Is* no such person?

PROFESSOR

Come. We'll talk on the plane.

THORNHILL

But I've been in his hotel room! I've tried on his clothes! He's got short sleeves and . . . and dandruff!

PROFESSOR

Believe me, Mr Thornhill, he doesn't exist. Which is why I'm going to have to ask *you* to go on *being* him for another twenty-four hours.

*Thornhill points a protesting finger at the Professor. Just as his mouth opens, there is the sudden roar of engines as a plane revs up and prepares to taxi away from the nearby ramp. Thornhill looks across at the plane with annoyance.*

THE PLANE

*As it starts to taxi away, its four engines creating a storm of noise and wind.*

MEDIUM LONG SHOT: THORNHILL AND THE PROFESSOR

*The two men are talking at each other, the Professor calmly, Thornhill gesticulating, arguing, denying, insisting, protesting. The Professor keeps tugging gently on Thornhill's arm, trying to move him along as he explains. As they start walking again, towards camera, they continue to talk to each other. We have heard none of this conversation, because distance from camera and the noise of the plane taxiing away have intervened . . . long enough for the Professor to give Thornhill a brief outline of the George Kaplan plan which we learned about in Washington. As the two men approach camera and walk through the gate on to the field, where another passenger plane stands waiting, the Professor appears to be making an appeal, and Thornhill is shaking his head vigorously. They have walked into a tighter two-shot and the sound of the taxiing plane has faded away. We can hear them now.*

#### THORNHILL

Look – you started this crazy decoy business without me! *Finish* it without me! . . .

#### PROFESSOR

And well we might have if you hadn't stumbled into it . . .

#### THORNHILL

. . . *I* think you should give me a *medal* and a *very* long *vacation* instead of asking me to go *on* being a target just so that your Number One, or whatever you call him, doesn't get shot at!

#### PROFESSOR

Not shot at, Mr Thornhill – *found out*. Once he's found out, he's as good as dead. And thanks to *you* clouds of suspicion *are* forming –

#### THORNHILL

Thanks to *me* – !

#### PROFESSOR

If you'll get on the plane –

#### THORNHILL

I'm an advertising man, not a red herring! I've got a job, a secretary, a mother, two ex-wives and several bartenders waiting for me, and I don't intend to disappoint them all and get myself slightly killed by playing the man in the gray-flannel cloak-and-dagger. The answer is no!

#### PROFESSOR

Is that final?

#### THORNHILL

Yes!

*The Professor looks at him for a moment, then holds out his hand.*

#### PROFESSOR

Goodbye then.
    (*as Thornhill takes the hand uncertainly*)
If I thought there was any chance of changing your mind, I'd talk about Miss Kendall, whom you obviously disapprove of for good reason . . .

                    THORNHILL
                     (*savagely*)
Yeah – for using sex like some people use a fly-swatter . . .
For trying to have me exterminated . . .

                    PROFESSOR
I don't suppose it would matter to you that she was probably
*forced* to do whatever she did . . . in order to protect herself.

                    THORNHILL
                  (*almost a sneer*)
Protect herself from *what*?

                    PROFESSOR
                     (*slowly*)
Suspicion . . . exposure . . . assassination.
                 (*Thornhill stares at him*)
Forgive me for referring to our Number One as a man, Mr
Thornhill. It's about all *I* can do to help keep her safe while
she's in all this terrible danger . . .

CLOSE SHOT: THORNHILL
*Turning to camera, eyes filled with emotion as he shakes his head*
*slowly, trying to throw off the pain of his confused feelings.*

                PROFESSOR'S VOICE
                   (*off-screen*)
I know you didn't mean to, but I'm afraid you *have* put her in
a most delicate situation – and much more than her life is at
stake . . .

*During this, another plane has been arriving, its landing lights slowly*
*increasing the illumination on Thornhill's stricken face and the*
*background behind him. The sound of the engines rises, as though*
*illustrating the mounting determination within Thornhill, and his*
*ultimate decision.*

    DISSOLVE TO:

LONG SHOT: THE PLANE IN FLIGHT – NIGHT

*We are shooting up at the plane from an elevation on the ground as it approaches camera in a slightly descending path. As the plane comes nearer and zooms past, camera pans with it slightly and discovers:*

THE FACES OF THE PRESIDENTS. MT RUSHMORE — NIGHT

*The monument glows against the night sky, lit by several banks of unseen searchlights. We hold on this shot. And then the fading sound of the disappearing plane slowly becomes the sound of laughter and many voices. Slowly, night turns to day.*

THE FACES OF THE PRESIDENTS — MT RUSHMORE — DAY

*Same angle as above. The searchlights have been replaced by sunlight. The black sky has turned blue. Camera pulls back slowly, until a circular border appears at the edges of the screen. We are in:*

EFFECT SHOT: THE FACES OF THE PRESIDENTS — AS SEEN THROUGH BINOCULARS

*As soon as we have established the binocular effect —*

    CUT TO:

CLOSE SHOT: THORNHILL — MT RUSHMORE OBSERVATION DECK

*We are on Thornhill's back as he stands peering through binoculars mounted on a pedestal. (There are similar glasses located at many vantage points throughout the park.)*

> THORNHILL

Suppose they don't come.

> PROFESSOR'S VOICE
> (*off-screen*)

They'll come.

*During this we have pulled back to reveal the Professor sitting nearby reading a Rapid City newspaper, his back half-turned away from Thornhill.*

> THORNHILL
> (*uneasily*)

I don't like the way Teddy Roosevelt is looking at me . . .

**PROFESSOR**

He's trying to give you one last word of caution, Mr Kaplan: speak softly, and carry a big stick.

*Thornhill leaves the binoculars, starts restlessly past the Professor to the corner of the terrace.*

**THORNHILL**

*I* think he's trying to tell me not to go through with this hair-brained scheme . . .

**PROFESSOR**

Perhaps he doesn't know to what extent *you* are the *cause* of our present difficulties –

**THORNHILL**
(*turning to him*)

I'm not so sure I *accept* that charge, Professor.

**PROFESSOR**
(*mildly*)

My dear fellow – if you had not made yourself so damnably attractive to Miss Kendall that she fell for you –

**THORNHILL**
(*momentarily delighted*)

And vice versa.

**PROFESSOR**

– Our friend Vandamm wouldn't be losing faith in her loyalty now. It was quite obvious to him last night that she had become emotionally involved, worst of all with a man he thinks is a government agent.

**THORNHILL**

Are you trying to tell me – *and* Teddy Roosevelt – that I'm irresistible?

**PROFESSOR**
(*sternly*)

I'm trying to remind you that it's *your* responsibility to help us restore her to Vandamm's good graces . . .
(*he sees Thornhill's face cloud over*)

. . . Right up to the moment he leaves the country tonight.

                            THORNHILL
                            (*annoyed*)
   All right. All right.
   (*he points a finger to remind the Professor of a previous bargain*)
   But after tonight . . .

                            PROFESSOR
                            (*looking away*)
   My blessings on you both.

*Thornhill nods. Then he looks off-screen and reacts tensely.*

                            THORNHILL
   Here they are.

*The Professor's nonchalance vanishes instantly. He gets up and walks
swiftly away. Thornhill looks off again.*

POINT OF VIEW: THE PARKING AREA
*A white Lincoln convertible is pulling into a parking space, comes to a
stop. The driver is Vandamm. Eve and Leonard sit beside him. They
get out of the car, glance about and start towards the cafeteria building.*

THORNHILL
*Watches them for a moment, then turns purposefully and hurries
towards the cafeteria from his level. We move with him either with a
dolly shot or a series of cuts, depending on the location of his starting
point.*

*(It will not always be specifically indicated, but it should be borne in
mind that the entire Mt Rushmore day sequence takes place with
sightseers, camera bugs, little children and assorted tourists in evidence
at all times, whether outdoors or indoors.)*

EXT. MT RUSHMORE CAFETERIA & GIFT SHOP BUILDING

*Thornhill approaches the building and enters.*

INT. BUILDING – MASTER SCENE

*Thornhill walks across the lobby to the cafeteria, a vast room with many tables and enormous windows through which can be seen the faces of the presidents in the distance. It is after the lunch hour, and only half of the tables are occupied. Thornhill goes over to the steam-table and asks for a cup of coffee. While waiting for it, he turns and looks towards the parking area entrance to the cafeteria. No one is coming through there yet. He receives the cup of coffee and starts towards an unoccupied table. Just as he arrives at the table, he sees Vandamm, Leonard and Eve enter the cafeteria. He remains standing until they see him. Then he sits down, as Vandamm and Eve walk towards him. Leonard sits down at a table near the entrance, as though he were a sentry standing guard in case of trouble.*

**AT THE TABLE**

*Vandamm and Eve arrive at the table. Eve has a strained look. Thornhill contemptuously refuses even to glance at her. His ignoring of her presence is his way of demonstrating to Vandamm how bitterly he despises her. (Thornhill is now playing a terse, matter-of-fact 'Kaplan' rather than his usual protesting self.)*

> **VANDAMM**
> *(with a mild smile)*
> Good afternoon, Mr Kaplan.

*He starts to draw out a chair for Eve.*

> **THORNHILL**
> *(sharply)*
> Not her.

*Vandamm's manner changes. He turns to Eve and, with a sharp incline of the head, dismisses her. Tight-lipped, Eve turns and walks off towards the gift shop. Thornhill looks after her with noticeable distaste. Vandamm sits down, resuming his deceptively polite manner.*

*(At times during the following, Thornhill will look past Vandamm towards the gift shop and we will see that Eve, 'browsing' in the gift shop, is standing right next to another 'browser', who could even be exchanging whispered words with her. It is the Professor. And if Leonard, seated near the doorway, would turn his head, he might even see them. But he does not turn his head. And he does not know the Professor.)*

**VANDAMM**

Did I misunderstand you about bringing her?

**THORNHILL**

We'll get to that.
> (*as he lights a cigarette*)

I suppose you were surprised to get my call . . .

**VANDAMM**

Not at all. I knew the police would release *you*, Mr Kaplan. By the way, I want to compliment you on your colorful exit from the auction gallery . . .

**THORNHILL**

Thank you.

**VANDAMM**

And now what little drama are we here for today? You see, I don't for a moment believe that you invited me to these gay surroundings in order to come to an arrangement . . . .

**THORNHILL**

Suppose I were to tell you that I not only know exactly what time you're leaving the country tonight, but also the latitude and longitude of your rendezvous, and your ultimate destination.

**VANDAMM**

> (*after a beat*)

You wouldn't care to carry my bags, would you?

**THORNHILL**

Maybe you'd like to know the price, just the same.

**VANDAMM**

Price?

**THORNHILL**

For doing nothing to stop you.

**VANDAMM**

> (*amused*)

How much did you have in mind?

THORNHILL

I want the girl . . .

*The geniality dies on Vandamm's face for a moment. Then he gives a little smile of understanding.*

(shakes his head, then speaks with bitterness)
I want her to get what's coming to her. You turn her over to *me* and I'll see that there's enough pinned on *her* to keep her uncomfortable for the rest of her life. In return, I'll look the other way tonight.

*Vandamm peers at him for a moment.*

VANDAMM

She really got under your skin, didn't she?

THORNHILL
(angrily)
We're not talking about my skin. We're talking about yours. I'm offering you a chance to save it . . .

VANDAMM

To *exchange* it . . .

THORNHILL

Put it any way you like.

VANDAMM

I'm curious, Mr Kaplan. How did you arrive at this deduction that my feelings for Miss Kendall might have deteriorated to the point where I would . . . trade her in for . . . a little peace of mind?

THORNHILL

I don't deduce. I observe.

*The two men stare at each other steadily. Then Vandamm looks up and gets to his feet.*

FULL SHOT: THE TABLE
*Eve is standing beside the table, her face tense. She doesn't look at Thornhill.*

148

EVE
(*coldly*)

Phillip – if you don't mind, I'm going back to the house.

*She immediately turns and starts to leave the cafeteria. Vandamm, momentarily caught off guard, looks after her hesitantly, and then, after a quick look at Thornhill, goes after her.*

CLOSE-UP: THORNHILL
*Looking off after them. He rises with concern on his face.*

POINT OF VIEW: FROM THORNHILL
*Vandamm has caught up with Eve. There is a brief unheard exchange between them, then Vandamm beckons Leonard over to them and the three start swiftly towards the exit.*

CLOSE SHOT: THORNHILL
*Seeing this turn of events and reacting to it, he starts after them.*

WIDER ANGLE (MASTER SCENE)
*Thornhill moves swiftly across the cafeteria to head off Vandamm, Eve and Leonard, who are approaching the door leading out to the parking area. Thornhill catches up with Eve, puts a hand on her.*

THORNHILL
(*quietly and tensely*)

Just a second, you.

*Vandamm and Leonard, a few steps ahead of her, stop and look back.*

EVE
(*mutters, pulling free*)

Get away from me!

*She goes towards the two men, who are starting to return. Thornhill grabs Eve by the arm, pulls her, struggling, back into the cafeteria.*

(*through her breath*)

Let go!

*Vandamm starts to make a move towards the struggling Eve and Thornhill. Leonard quickly stays him. All of this takes place with lightning rapidity. Vandamm watches tensely.*

Let *go* of me!

**THORNHILL**

You're not going anywhere . . .
> (*he pulls her violently away from the others*)

*Come* on . . .

*The camera moves in for a close-up of Vandamm. From his point of view, we see the struggling couple.*

**EVE**

No! . . . Please! . . .

**THORNHILL**

Save the phoney tears . . .

*She breaks out of his grasp, backs away. He comes towards her, stops suddenly. She has taken her automatic from her handbag, points it at him.*

**EVE**

Get back . . .

**THORNHILL**

You little fool . . .

*He starts slowly towards her. She backs towards the entrance, eyes wide with terror.*

**EVE**

Stay away from me . . .

*Thornhill lunges at her. She fires at him once. He clutches his chest, stops dead in his tracks. She fires again. He spins, crashes into a table and falls to the floor. Crowds scream. Pandemonium ensues. Eve dashes out past Vandamm, who starts to follow, but Leonard restrains him.*

**LEONARD**

No good, sir. You can't get involved in this.

**IN A SERIES OF QUICK CUTS:**
*1 The Professor is seen running across the cafeteria towards Thornhill's fallen body.*

*2 Eve is seen running down the path towards the parking area.*

3 *Leonard is seen unobtrusively escorting Vandamm to the back of the crowd.*

4 *The Professor is seen pushing his way through the crowds surrounding Thornhill's body, saying: 'Get back! Please! Don't touch anything!'*

5 *Eve is seen getting into Vandamm's car, gunning the motor, speeding away.*

6 *Leonard is seen moving up to the edge of the crowd surrounding Thornhill's body, maneuvering himself into position until he can see:*

7 *The Professor kneeling over Thornhill's body, feeling the heart. He withdraws his hands, wipes blood from his fingers with a handkerchief and looks up gravely as a shocked murmur arises from the onlookers and one woman begins to cry.*

    QUICK DISSOLVE TO:

EXT. DRIVEWAY ENTRANCE TO PARK — FEW MINUTES LATER

*Shooting over the heads of hushed onlookers in foreground, we see two green-uniformed park attendants bearing Thornhill on a stretcher to the rear of a parked hospital van. Several men remove their hats as the stretcher goes by. The Professor is on hand to supervise as the stretcher is placed in the van and the rear doors are shut. Now the Professor gets in the front seat beside the driver, and the van drives off.*

QUICK DISSOLVE TO:

EXT. SECLUDED ROAD — A FEW MINUTES LATER

*Camera is on a lovely wooded glen securely hidden from the main road that cuts through the Black Hills. Perhaps the Mt Rushmore monument can be seen in the distance through the trees. Camera pans over, revealing the parked ambulance. The Professor is in the act of opening the back doors. He peers in.*

PROFESSOR

Mr Thornhill . . .

*Thornhill rises with alacrity.*

THORNHILL

Are we there?

PROFESSOR

No.

*Thornhill looks off, sees someone and slides out of the ambulance to his feet. He stands for a moment looking off. Then, as he starts slowly forward, camera eases back ultimately to reveal Eve standing beside the white Lincoln convertible. During this, the Professor has started back towards the front of the ambulance, saying:*

Don't be long.

*Thornhill and Eve regard each other uncertainly as she starts moving towards him. Camera now eases in, ultimately to a two shot.*

*They continue to gaze at each other uncertainly. In a way, they are meeting for the first time, for it is the first time that they are together with Thornhill knowing who Eve is and with Eve aware that Thornhill knows who she is. (The play-acting scene at the cafeteria did not count, for they were prevented from acknowledging the true situation.) After all that Eve has done to Thornhill and he has said to her, neither can be certain of the other's true feelings. It is a time for uneasiness, caution and tentative probing – eventually giving way*

152

to what has always been apparent: the fact that they do like each other more than somewhat.

                                  EVE

Hello . . .

                              THORNHILL

Hello . . .

*A moment of silence.*

                                  EVE

Are you all right?

                              THORNHILL

Yes. I think so.

*More silence. They move closer.*

                                  EVE

I asked the Professor to let me see you again . . .

                              THORNHILL

Oh?

*He waits.*

                                  EVE

There isn't . . . much time . . .

                              THORNHILL
                            (*non-committal*)

Isn't there?

                                  EVE

I . . . wanted to tell you . . . I mean . . . apologize . . .

                              THORNHILL
                            (*without feeling*)

No need. I understand . . .
                             (*slightly bitter*)
All in the line of duty . . .

                                  EVE

I did treat you miserably . . .

THORNHILL
(*a self-accusation*)

I hated you for it . . .

EVE
(*faltering*)

And I didn't want you to . . . go on . . . thinking . . .

THORNHILL
(*softening slightly*)

I used some pretty harsh words. I'm . . . sorry . . .

EVE

They hurt . . . deeply . . .

THORNHILL
(*defensively*)

Naturally, if I'd known . . .

EVE
(*defensively*)

I couldn't tell you . . .

THORNHILL

No . . .

EVE

Could I?

THORNHILL

Of course not.

*Eve gives the tiniest of shrugs. They gaze at each other. That is the whole situation. Nobody to blame really. No need for further apologies. They each were unkind to the other – but always with due cause. But mixed in with the unkind acts and harsh words had been other acts, other words, other feelings – no? Eve smiles at him tenderly.*

EVE

You didn't get hurt. I'm so relieved.

THORNHILL
(*eagerly*)

Of course I was hurt. How would *you* have felt if – ?

154

EVE

I mean when you fell in the cafeteria, when I – bang bang –
shot you.

THORNHILL
(*smiles*)

Oh, that . . . No.

EVE
(*moving closer*)

You did it rather well, I thought.

THORNHILL
(*pleased with himself*)

Yes – I was quite . . . graceful . . .

EVE
(*putting her hands on him*)

Considering that it's not really your kind of work . . .

THORNHILL
(*touching her tenderly*)

I got into it by accident. What's *your* excuse?

EVE

I met Phillip Vandamm at a party one night and saw only his
charm. I guess I had nothing to do that weekend, so I decided
to fall in love . . .

THORNHILL
(*sorry he brought the whole thing up*)

That's nice.

EVE

Eventually, the Professor and his Washington colleagues
approached me with a few sordid details about Phillip and
told me that my . . . *relationship* with him made me 'uniquely
valuable' to them.

THORNHILL
(*bridling*)

So *you* turned Girl Scout.

#### EVE

Maybe it was the first time anyone ever asked me to do anything worthwhile.

#### THORNHILL

Has life been like that?

#### EVE

Mm hmmm.

#### THORNHILL

How come?

#### EVE

Men like you.

#### THORNHILL
(*kissing her*)

What's wrong with men like me?

#### EVE

They don't believe in marriage.

#### THORNHILL

I've been married twice.

#### EVE

See what I mean?

*He looks at her with affection.*

#### THORNHILL

Y'know something. I may go back to hating you again. It was more fun.

#### EVE
(*with a trace of sadness*)

You're not going to have the chance. There isn't time.
(*she gives him a quick embrace*)
Goodbye, Thornhill.

#### THORNHILL
(*holding her*)

Wait a minute. Not so soon.

#### EVE

I have to get back to the house and convince them I took the long way around so nobody would follow me there.

#### THORNHILL
(*holding her even closer*)

Can't we just stand like this for a few more hours?

#### EVE

You're supposed to be critically wounded.

#### THORNHILL

I never felt more alive.

#### EVE

Whose side are you on?

#### THORNHILL

Yours, always.

#### EVE

Then don't undermine my resolve, just when I need it most.

*They hear the short beep of a horn and look off. The Professor is motioning to Thornhill to come.*

#### THORNHILL

I guess it's off to the hospital for *me* . . .
(*they start walking slowly*)
. . . And back to danger for you. I don't like it one bit.

#### EVE

Much safer now, thanks to you, my darling decoy.

#### THORNHILL

Don't thank me. I couldn't stand it.

#### EVE

All right. I won't.

#### THORNHILL

And just as soon as your malevolent friend Vandamm takes off tonight, I'm going to undo my bandages, and you and I are going to do a lot of apologizing to each other, in private . . .

**EVE**
(*glancing at him wistfully*)

Don't talk like that . . .

**THORNHILL**

It's the way I feel . . .

**EVE**

You mustn't . . .

**THORNHILL**

I must . . .

**EVE**

You know it can't be.

**THORNHILL**
(*unconcerned*)

Of course it can be.

*Eve stops, looks up at him, disturbed. She glances towards the Professor.*

**EVE**

He *has* told you, hasn't he?

**THORNHILL**
(*puzzled*)

Told me what?

*Eve shakes her head, unable to speak.*

**PROFESSOR**
(*coming up to them*)

Miss Kendall – you've *got* to get moving . . .

**EVE**
(*with a final embrace*)

Goodbye, Thornhill . . .

**THORNHILL**
(*holding on to her*)

Wait a minute . . .
(*to the Professor*)
*What* didn't you tell me?

158

*Eve and the Professor glance at each other. There are tears in Eve's eyes now.*

#### EVE

Why didn't you?

*For a brief moment, the Professor's face reveals an all-too-human regret for what he has done. Then he looks at Thornhill and speaks crisply.*

#### PROFESSOR

She's going off with Vandamm tonight on the plane.

#### THORNHILL
(*stunned*)

Going off with Vandamm?

#### PROFESSOR

That's why we've gone to such lengths to make her a fugitive from justice – so that Vandamm couldn't very well decline to take her along –

#### THORNHILL

But you said –

#### PROFESSOR

I needn't tell you how valuable she can be to us over there.

#### THORNHILL

You lied to me! You said after tonight – !

#### PROFESSOR

I needed your help . . . .

#### THORNHILL
(*bitterly*)

Well, *you got* it all right . . . .

#### EVE
(*through tears*)

Don't be angry . . . .

#### THORNHILL
(*to Eve*)

If you think I'm going to let you go through with this dirty business – !

PROFESSOR

She has to.

THORNHILL
(*turning on him*)

Nobody has to do anything! I don't like the games you play,
Professor – !

PROFESSOR

War is hell, Mr Thornhill – even when it's a cold one.

THORNHILL
(*savagely*)

– If you fellows can't lick the Vandamms without asking girls
like her to bed down with them and fly away with them and
probably never come back alive, maybe you better start
learning to *lose* a few cold wars!

PROFESSOR
(*quietly*)

I'm afraid we're already doing that.

*Suddenly Eve breaks away, runs for her car. Thornhill goes after her,
and the Professor quickly motions to the ambulance driver to step down.*

**AT THE CAR**
*Eve gets into the car, starts the motor, as Thornhill catches up with her
and pulls open the door to stop her.*

THORNHILL

I'm not going to let you . . .

EVE

Don't spoil everything now . . . please . . .

THORNHILL

Come on – *out* . . .

*A hand taps him on the back. He turns.*

**CLOSE SHOT: THE AMBULANCE DRIVER**
*His fist is cocked, and moving on the backward arc of a knockout
punch.*

CUT TO:

**CLOSE SHOT: THE CAR DOOR**
*Slamming shut as though it were illustrating the impact of fist on jaw.*
*The car drives off with a screech of tires, and we see Thornhill falling*
*into the shot, and to the ground.*

DISSOLVE TO:

**INT. HOSPITAL ROOM – NIGHT**

*Start close on a bedside radio. During broadcast pull back to reveal*
*Thornhill in trousers and undershirt. His jacket, tie and red-stained shirt*
*hang nearby. He is pacing back and forth, nervously smoking a*
*cigarette.*

RADIO ANNOUNCER'S VOICE
– in full view of scores of horrified men, women and children
who had come to the park to see the famed Mt Rushmore
monument. Witnesses to the shooting described Kaplan's
assailant as an attractive blonde in her late twenties. Kaplan,
who was removed to the Rapid City Hospital in critical
condition, has been tentatively identified as an employee of
the Federal Government . . . The tragedy developed with
startling suddenness. Chris Swenson, a busboy in the Mt
Rushmore cafeteria, stated that he heard voices raised in what
seemed to be –

*Thornhill angrily switches off the radio and snuffs out his cigarette in an*
*ashtray with a violent thrust. He goes to the single window which is*
*open, stares down at the street many stories below. He turns, walks*
*towards the door, feeling his jaw and wincing with pain. He pulls at the*
*doorknob, knowing it is locked but unable to resist giving it another try.*
*Impatiently he hits at the unyielding door as though it were his enemy.*
*He is locked in, and quite obviously he'd like to be out. He begins to*
*pace the room again. Now he hears footsteps approaching in the*
*hallway outside, then a key in the lock. Quickly, and with noticeable*
*cunning, he lies down on the bed. The door opens and the Professor*
*walks in carrying a brand-new white shirt.*

PROFESSOR
(*handing him the shirt*)

Here we are. Sixteen and three-quarter collar, thirty-five sleeves, no ketchup stains.

THORNHILL

Thanks.

*He starts to put on the shirt.*

PROFESSOR

How are you feeling?

THORNHILL

All right – considering that your driver was born with a sledgehammer instead of a hand.

PROFESSOR

Sorry about that.

THORNHILL
(*pretending*)

No. I deserved it.
(*gesturing towards the door*)
And that locked door too . . .

PROFESSOR

If you were seen wandering about in good health, it could prove fatal to Miss Kendall . . .

THORNHILL

No need to lock me in anymore.

PROFESSOR

Good.

THORNHILL

I've been acting childish . . .

*Thornhill turns away from the Professor and we see on his face that he has ulterior motives.*

PROFESSOR

We all do at times, where a woman is concerned.

**THORNHILL**

I've already started to forget her.

**PROFESSOR**

Good . . .

**THORNHILL**

Yes.

**PROFESSOR**

Better that way.

**THORNHILL**

Much.

**PROFESSOR**

Inside of an hour she'll be gone.

*Thornhill has to tighten his lips to keep from showing anything to the Professor other than utter lack of interest.*

**THORNHILL**

How goes it in the world outside?

**PROFESSOR**

Fine. Mr Kaplan's untimely shooting has now acquired the authority of the printed word. Enormous headlines. Everyone has been cooperating beautifully.

**THORNHILL**

You may now include *me*.

**PROFESSOR**

I'm most grateful.

**THORNHILL**

A favor in return?

**PROFESSOR**

Anything.

**THORNHILL**

A bottle of scotch. A pint'll do.

**PROFESSOR**

May I join you?

**THORNHILL**

Wonderful. Make it a quart.

*The Professor goes to the door, opens it and looks back.*

**PROFESSOR**

See you in a few minutes.

*Thornhill smiles, the picture of friendly cooperation. The door closes softly. And almost before it has clicked shut, Thornhill's smile disappears. He seizes his jacket, struggles into it, closes his collar at the neck, stuffs his tie into his pocket and steps to the door. He turns the knob and pulls. To his surprise and dismay, the door is locked. The Professor has been one step ahead of him.*

**THORNHILL**
*(with disgust)*

Why, the dirty sneak.

*He looks around, glances at his wrist-watch, makes a decision, goes to the window and looks down at the street below. Then he takes a deep breath, swallows his fear and climbs out onto the ledge.*

**THE LEDGE**
*Thornhill inches his way along the shallow ledge until he comes to another window, partially open. He raises it as silently as he can and starts to climb in.*

**INT. ANOTHER HOSPITAL ROOM**

*The room is in darkness. Thornhill's silhouette is framed in the window as he climbs in. As his feet touch the floor, a light suddenly comes on. An attractive Brunette has switched on the lamp on the night-table and now sits up in bed. Thornhill holds a finger to his lips, starts towards the bed (and the door beyond).*

**BRUNETTE**

Stop!

**THORNHILL**
*(softly, as he walks by)*

Excuse me.

*The woman quickly takes her harlequin glasses from the night-table, puts them on and looks at Thornhill as he goes past the bed and continues on to the door.*

BRUNETTE
*(in an entirely different tone of voice)*

    Stop . . .

*Thornhill opens the door and walks out on the invitation.*

    DISSOLVE TO:

EXT. ROAD BEYOND MT RUSHMORE – NIGHT

*A taxi is speeding along a winding dirt road.*

ANOTHER ANGLE
*The cab slows down and comes to a stop near the beginning of a high stone wall.*

CLOSER SHOT
*As Thornhill gets out of the cab, the driver turns to him.*

DRIVER

    Sure you don't want me to take you right up there?

THORNHILL

    No. This is fine.

*The cab drives off.*

THORNHILL
*He looks about, then moves along the wall until he comes to a pair of heavy iron gates – the only entrance to the area beyond the wall. The gates are open. He goes through and sees:*

ESTABLISHING SHOT: VANDAMM'S HOUSE
*It is a sprawling modern structure in the Frank Lloyd Wright tradition set on a rise in the land at the end of a long driveway. Lights are ablaze. There is evidence of activity within.*

**ANOTHER ANGLE: WITH THORNHILL**
*Cautiously he approaches the house and makes his way around to the back. The terrain there is rocky and slopes sharply down to a level field. The house juts out over this slope, cantilever style. As Thornhill stands in the dark looking about, he suddenly sees:*

**THE FIELD BEHIND THE HOUSE**
*Two parallel rows of lights several hundred yards long. They are very clearly the runway lights of a hidden landing strip. They flash off and on again, as though being tested, and then the field falls back into darkness.*

**ANOTHER ANGLE: WITH THORNHILL**
*He turns around and starts up the slope, moving to his right towards the side of the house where the incline is less steep. Just as he reaches the house, he stops, on the alert, as he hears the sound of an approaching car. He looks off, sees:*

**POINT OF VIEW**
*The headlights of the approaching car sweep along the driveway, and then the car itself is seen coming around the side of the house and pulling to a stop in the parking area. It is a small sedan. The driver gets out. It is Valerian. He is carrying a newspaper. At this moment, a side door of the house opens and a woman walks out to meet Valerian. It is the housekeeper last seen at the Townsend estate in Glen Cove. Together, they go towards the house, moving directly towards Thornhill.*

**THORNHILL**
*He quickly ducks beneath the cantilevered portion of the house and hides. He hears a door opening and closing, then footsteps and voices inside the house above him, the sound coming through the floor. Thornhill glances about, then decides to climb up one of the cantilevers. This will enable him to get a view of what might be going on inside the house. All the time that he has been underneath the house, he has been hearing a mumble of voices from above. He moves forward.*

**ANOTHER ANGLE: EXT. HOUSE**
*Thornhill appears from beneath the house, groping his way up the diagonal beam of the cantilever and then climbing up onto the*

*horizontal beam. He is now outside one of the large windows of the living-room. A section of the window is open. With cat-like stealth he moves along the cantilever towards the window, takes up a position in the shadows and peers inside.*

INT. LIVING-ROOM – FROM THORNHILL

*A large room, strikingly furnished, and dominated by a great chandelier which hangs suspended from the two-story-high beamed ceiling. A stairway at the far end leads to a balcony which runs the length of the room. Off this balcony are bedrooms. In foreground near the window is a table on which can be seen some effects of Vandamm – a black briefcase, books strapped together, boxes of his favorite cigarettes, and the pre-Columbian figure, the Tarascan warrior, purchased at the auction. Vandamm and Eve are near the bar. Close to them is an opened newspaper. Eve appears strained. (Her parting with Thornhill has threatened her self-control considerably.) Vandamm, assuming that she is upset over the shooting, has been trying to comfort her in a soothing, gentle voice.*

VANDAMM
– Nothing to worry about –

EVE
– I lost my head –

*During following, Leonard enters in background unobserved by them. He watches them with a curious smirk on his face, as though he were in possession of a delightful secret unknown to anyone but him.*

VANDAMM
I'm not just saying this to make you feel better, my dear. I mean it . . .

EVE
I didn't know what I was doing . . .

VANDAMM
He was going to destroy you. You had to protect yourself . . .

EVE
But not endanger *you* . . .

167

**VANDAMM**

Nonsense. There's not a word, not a whisper that links you or me, *any* of us, with this thing. There would have been *some* hint on the radio or in the paper. Look for yourself.

**EVE**
(*shaking her head*)

I don't want to look . . .

**VANDAMM**
(*with sympathy*)

Or even think about it. I can understand that.
(*he takes her face in his hands*)
Will you ever forgive me, my dear?

**EVE**

Forgive you?

**VANDAMM**

For upsetting you so . . . for not showing more confidence in your devotion . . .

**EVE**
(*a wan smile*)

Dear Phillip . . .

**VANDAMM**

Soon we'll be off together, and I shall dedicate myself to your happiness.

*He kisses her gently, then turns towards Leonard.*

What's the situation, Leonard?

**LEONARD**
(*facetiously*)

About the plane, you mean?

**VANDAMM**

Of course. What was the last report?

**LEONARD**

Over Whitestone on the hour. Six thousand. Descending.

VANDAMM

Another ten minutes.

LEONARD

At the most.

VANDAMM

Bags?

LEONARD

Outside.

VANDAMM

Runway lights?

LEONARD

Checked.

VANDAMM

Good.

LEONARD

And now, I wonder if I could have a few words of parting with you, sir?

Certainly.

LEONARD

*(looking at Eve)*

In private?

*Vandamm glances sharply at Leonard. Eve senses tension, quickly relieves the situation.*

EVE

I'll go upstairs and get my things.

*She starts up the stairs.*

OUTSIDE THE WINDOW

*Thornhill watches as Eve goes up to the balcony. Leonard stares at her all the way, and Vandamm peers at* him, *sensing hostility in his attitude. When Eve disappears into one of the bedrooms, Vandamm addresses Leonard with a trace of facetiousness.*

VANDAMM

Well, Leonard – how does one say farewell to one's own right arm?

LEONARD

In your case, sir, I'm afraid you're going to wish you had cut it off sooner . . .

*During the above interchange, Thornhill will glance sharply up to his right when he sees the lights go on in the balcony bedroom window, and then Eve herself appear for a moment at the window.* The voices in the living-room dwindle to an unintelligible drone *as Thornhill backs away from the open living-room window towards the end of the cantilever beam. He is now in a better position to attract Eve's attention. He glances about for a pebble to throw, but he is too far above ground to reach one. He takes a coin from his pocket, glances cautiously towards the living-room, then looks up and throws the coin at Eve's window. It hits noisily and falls to the ground below.*

INTERCUT SEVERAL ANGLES

*Eve appears at the window, looks out for a moment, then walks away.*

*Thornhill takes another coin from his pocket, throws it at the window and hits again.*

*Eve appears at the window, opens it and looks out.*

*Just as Thornhill starts to call to her, he glances sharply towards the living-room.*

*Leonard is walking briskly over to the open living-room window. In a moment he will see Thornhill.*

*Thornhill ducks back into the shadows against the house.*

*Leonard peers out of the living-room window to see the cause of the noise he had heard; Eve continues to look out of the bedroom window. Thornhill cannot move out to signal her. Seeing nothing, Eve closes the window again and walks away.*

*Thornhill glances towards the living-room window and his eyes widen:*

*Leonard has moved away from the window and, with his back to Vandamm, is taking a gun from his pocket and placing it on a table near the window, as Vandamm talks in background, his words unintelligible.*

*Thornhill edges up to the window, as Leonard turns around, the gun concealed on the table behind him. The dialogue becomes intelligible again.*

INTERCUT INT. LIVING-ROOM & CLOSE-UPS OF THORNHILL LISTENING

LEONARD

You must have had *some* doubts about her yourself, and *still do* –

VANDAMM
(*disturbed, and trying to conceal it*)
Rubbish . . .

LEONARD
– Why else would you have decided not to tell her that our little treasure here . . .
(*patting the figure of the Tarascan warrior*)

171

. . . has a bellyfull of microfilm?

**VANDAMM**
(*angrily*)
*You* seem to be trying to fill *mine* with rotten apples.

**LEONARD**
Sometimes the truth does taste like a mouthful of worms, sir.

**VANDAMM**
(*snorts*)
What truth? I've heard nothing but innuendoes.

**LEONARD**
Call it my woman's intuition if you will, but I've never trusted neatness. Neatness is always the result of deliberate planning.

**VANDAMM**
(*defensively*)
She shot him in a moment of fear and anger. You were there. You saw it.

(*nods*)

And thereby wrapped everything up into one very neat and
tidy bundle:

*During the preceding speech, he picks up the gun, holds it behind his
back and advances further into the room, the camera following through
the window.*

    A. She removed any doubts you might have had about – what
did you call it? – her *'devotion'* and B. She gave herself a new
and *urgent* reason to be taken over to the other side with you,
just in *case* you decided to change your mind.

*Vandamm manages a laugh, but it is not very convincing.*

### VANDAMM
You know what *I* think? I think you're jealous of her. I mean
it. And I'm touched, dear boy. Really touched.

*Suddenly Leonard brings the gun out from behind his back and points it
at the startled Vandamm.*
(*sharply*)
Leonard!

*Leonard pulls the trigger, fires point blank at Vandamm. There is a
sharp report. Vandamm stands there, stunned but unharmed.*

### LEONARD
(*softly*)
The gun she shot Kaplan with. I found it in her luggage.

WAIST SHOT: VANDAMM
*The camera is very high, looking down on him. As the full realization of
what this means sinks in, the camera slowly descends to examine his
expression, and the angle becomes a big head. Vandamm's reaction is
carefully controlled. He is too big a man to let Leonard see the
humiliation and anger he feels at having been duped by Eve.*

### LEONARD'S VOICE
(*during above*)
It's an old Gestapo trick. Shoot one of your own people to

show that you're not one of them. They've just freshened it
up a bit with blank cartridges.

*Vandamm gives a little sigh.*

#### VANDAMM

What a pity . . .

*From upstairs, the sound of a door opening. Vandamm looks up, and
his brooding expression quickly changes to a wistful smile.*

Ready, dear?

CLOSE SHOT: EVE
*Standing at the balcony railing looking down at him.*

#### EVE

I thought I heard a shot . . .

FULL SHOT: THE LIVING-ROOM

#### VANDAMM
(*calmly*)

Yes . . . so did we . . .
        (*moves towards the window*)
Must have been a car backfiring or something.
        (*looks out*)
Hurry down, pet. Almost time to go.

#### EVE

In a moment.

*She goes back into her room. Leonard moves at Vandamm, speaking in
a harsh voice.*

#### LEONARD

You're not taking her on that plane with you?

#### VANDAMM

Of course I am.

*Leonard stares at him. Vandamm looks back at him the way an adult
looks at a small boy.*

Like our friends, I too believe in neatness, Leonard.

This matter is best disposed of from a great height . . . over
water.

CLOSE SHOT: THORNHILL
*Aghast at what he has heard.*

WIDER ANGLE
*Thornhill backs away from the open window, looks up at Eve's
bedroom. The light is still on. Inside the living-room, Valerian has
entered in background and is receiving instructions from Vandamm.
Leonard has taken up a position near the open window. Even if he
thought it would do any good, Thornhill would not dare hurl another
coin at Eve's window now. His lips tighten. He makes a decision, starts
to climb up the side of the house to her room.*

CLOSE ANGLE: THORNHILL
*The camera follows him as he makes his way precariously up the side of
the house. Eve's window is beyond him and always in view. We see her
moving about and putting on her things during his climb. There is little
on which Thornhill can gain purchase as he climbs, little to hang on to.
He cuts his hand. Several times he almost crashes to disaster. The last
few feet are the hardest. He claws his way to the window sill of Eve's
bedroom, grabs it with his left hand, pulls himself up, gets his right hand
working, and with a final gasp, gets his body up high enough to be able
to see through the closed window into the room. Just as his head clears
the sill, the lights in the room go out and, over his shoulder, we see Eve
silhouetted in the doorway,* walking out.

INT. BEDROOM

*Thornhill, outside the window, stares dejectedly through the glass, then
silently works the window open. He climbs into the room and stands
there for a moment in the semi-darkness catching his breath. He looks at
his cut hand, takes out his handkerchief and presses it into the bleeding
palm. Then he steps cautiously to the doorway and looks out over the
living-room below. He cannot see much of the room because of the
balcony, and his unfavorable vantage point. But he can hear voices:*

175

How about a little champagne before we go?

EVE'S VOICE

I'd love it.

VANDAMM'S VOICE
(*after he walks to bar*)
It may not be cold enough.

EVE'S VOICE

Over the rocks will be all right.

VANDAMM'S VOICE

Really?

EVE'S VOICE

Sure.

VANDAMM'S VOICE

Good idea.

*Suddenly Thornhill glances back towards the open window, alarmed at what he hears – the first faint drone of an approaching plane. He looks about desperately, not knowing what to do. His eyes fall on the handkerchief still held in his hand. He sees his monogram: 'ROT' on the cloth. He glances towards the doorway, and an idea is born. He feels in his side pocket and takes out a match folder.* (In an insert, we see that the match folder is the same one he and Eve discussed at dinner on the train. It bears his personal trademark: ROT.) *He takes a pen from his pocket, opens the match folder and writes a message on the inside of the cover:* 'THEY'RE ON TO YOU! COME UP TO YOUR ROOM!' *He closes the folder, goes to the doorway and moves cautiously out to the balcony.*

HIGH ANGLE
*Shooting down over Thornhill in foreground as he edges forwards on the balcony, we see more of the living-room below. Eve is seated on the arm of a sofa. Her handbag is on the coffee table. Vandamm is turning away from the bar, walking towards her with a glass of champagne on the rocks in each hand. He gives her one, and they click glasses.*

**VANDAMM**

To you, my dear . . . and all the lovely moments we've had together . . .

**EVE**

Thank you, Phillip.

*As they drink, Leonard enters, walks towards the window.*

**LEONARD**

He's circling.

*Vandamm turns away from Eve, starts towards Leonard and the window.* At this, Thornhill tosses the folder of matches down at Eve. Just as he does so, she takes a sip of champagne and fails to see the folder land on the floor nearby.

LOW ANGLE: IN LIVING-ROOM

**VANDAMM**
(*to Leonard*)

Jump in. The champagne is fine.

**LEONARD**

There isn't time.

**VANDAMM**
(*ruefully*)

You always *were* a spoilsport, weren't you?

**LEONARD**
(*starting past him towards Eve*)

One of my most valuable attributes, as it now turns out.

*Automatically he stoops down and picks up the match folder lying on the floor, playing with it idly as he addresses Eve.* (*Thornhill watches in agony.*)

It would please me if you would think of me as being along on this journey, if only in spirit . . .

**EVE**

I shall, Leonard

*Leonard tosses the match folder to the coffee table before her and turns away, so that she cannot see his harsh expression. Eve sets her glass down on the coffee table as the sound of the plane grows louder.* And then she sees the match folder.

CLOSE-UP: EVE
*For a moment she is puzzled. Then her glance goes to the floor where she had seen Leonard pick up the matches. Realization begins to dawn on her.*

VANDAMM'S VOICE
(*off-screen*)

Come along, Eve.

EVE

All right . . .

*She gets to her feet, takes a cigarette from the coffee table, puts it between her lips and takes up the matches. We are very close as she opens the folder and reads* Thornhill's message *while striking a match and lighting the cigarette.*

ANOTHER ANGLE
*She looks up, sees the two men standing there waiting for her. She starts towards them, then suddenly feels her ear.*

EVE

Oh, I think I left my earrings upstairs . . .

*Before they can say anything, she runs right past them and up the stairs, clutching the match folder tightly.*

Be right down.

*Vandamm and Leonard glance at each other, then look towards her as she goes upstairs.*

POINT OF VIEW: FROM MEN
*Eve going up the stairs and along the balcony to her room.*

CLOSE SHOT: VANDAMM AND LEONARD
*Watching her.*

*Thornhill draws back into the bedroom as he sees Eve coming. She runs into the room, snaps on the light. He grabs her and pulls her towards the window as they speak in very fast, urgent whispers.*

> THORNHILL
>
> Quick! We can make it through the window! There's a car downstairs!

> EVE
> *(struggling)*
> Get away from here, you *idiot*! You'll ruin everything!

> THORNHILL
>
> Ruin everything? They know all about the fake shooting! They're going to do away with you!

> EVE
>
> What're you talking about?

> THORNHILL
>
> Leonard found the gun in your luggage! *You* heard the shot! . . .

*Eve stares at him, then glances quickly towards the door as she hears footsteps on the stairs.*

> . . . And I heard them say the figure they bought at the auction last night is filled with microfilm!

*Eve turns, looks at Thornhill.*

> EVE
>
> So that's how he's been getting the information.

> LEONARD'S VOICE
> *(from balcony)*
> Miss Kendall?

*She breaks away and goes quickly towards the door.*

> THORNHILL
> *(calling after her)*
> Don't get on that plane! I'll get the car!

*She snaps off the light and hurries out to:*

**THE BALCONY**
*— Just in time to head off Leonard, who has reached the top of the stairs. She closes the bedroom door behind her and goes quickly towards him. He stops, waits for her and they both start down the stairs.*

**THE LIVING-ROOM**
*As Eve and Leonard descend the stairs, Vandamm is talking in a reassuring tone of voice to the Housekeeper, who appears troubled.*

> VANDAMM

Don't worry, Anna. Arrangements have been made. You and your husband will be over the Canadian border by morning.

> HOUSEKEEPER

Thank you, sir.

> VANDAMM

Be careful now.

> HOUSEKEEPER

We will, sir. And God bless you.

*Vandamm turns and picks up the pre-Columbian figure while Leonard crosses over and picks up the briefcase, the books and the cigarettes. Eve's glance is on the figure held by Vandamm as he comes over to her. The three of them now start out through the exit door under the stairs as the Housekeeper starts up the room. As the Housekeeper goes out of the picture we see the balcony bedroom door open and Thornhill cautiously stepping forward and looking out.*

**POINT OF VIEW**
*The Housekeeper is retreating towards the other end of the room.*

**CLOSE SHOT: THE HOUSEKEEPER**
*Her walk slows up as she sees:*

**INSERT: A TURNED OFF TELEVISION SET**
*It reflects Thornhill standing on the distant balcony behind her.*

**CLOSE SHOT: PROFILE OF HOUSEKEEPER**
*She is still walking slowly. She turns her head ever so slightly, conscious of Thornhill's presence, and then makes her way around a corner out of sight.*

**CLOSE SHOT: THORNHILL**
*Satisfied that the woman is gone, he goes quickly along the balcony and down the stairs, camera following. As he reaches the bottom step, he hears:*

**HOUSEKEEPER'S VOICE**
Stay where you are!

*Thornhill turns, startled and sees:*

**POINT OF VIEW**
*The Housekeeper slowly advancing towards him from the far end of the room. She is holding a gun, pointed at him.*

**WIDER ANGLE**
*She stops within a few yards of him, motions towards a nearby chair.*

**HOUSEKEEPER**
Sit down.
                    (*Thornhill sits*)
As soon as the plane leaves, Mr Leonard and my husband will be back.

*Thornhill looks desperately towards the exit door.*

**EXT. HOUSE – DOLLY SHOT**
*Eve, Vandamm and Leonard have emerged from the house and are walking away from it towards the landing strip. Vandamm is holding Eve's arm. Leonard is walking behind them. They look off as they see:*

**REVERSE ANGLE: MOVING POINT OF VIEW**
*A twin-engined plane is letting down at the far end of the lighted runway, its landing lights ablaze.*

**EVE, VANDAMM AND LEONARD – DOLLY SHOT**
*The group are continuing their walk towards the plane. Now camera moves in to a close shot of Eve, as she walks. We see her anxious expression. The camera eases away to a three shot, and Eve's expression changes to a simulated nonchalant one.*

**CLOSE-UP: EVE**
*She looks over her shoulder, back towards the house.*

**POINT OF VIEW: THE HOUSE**
*No sign of Thornhill.*

**THREE SHOT**
*Vandamm is looking at Eve as she turns forward again.*

> **VANDAMM**
> What is it?

> **EVE**
> *(vaguely)*
> I was wondering about those earrings . . .

> **VANDAMM**
> They'll turn up.

*Camera eases in close on Eve again as she continues to walk. On her face we see increasing apprehension. She looks ahead.*

**POINT OF VIEW**
*The landed plane is taxiing towards the group. The silhouetted figure of Valerian is seen standing beside the baggage at the end of the runway.*

**ANOTHER ANGLE**
*The plane comes to a stop; the group arrives, and the cabin door is immediately opened from the inside. As Valerian starts to pass the baggage up to the man inside –*

> CUT TO:

**CLOSE-UP: EVE**
*She looks back towards the house with desperation.*

**POINT OF VIEW: THE HOUSE**
*Still no sign of Thornhill.*

**AT THE PLANE**
*While Valerian continues to dispose of the luggage, Vandamm, still holding Eve by the arm, turns to Leonard.*

> VANDAMM
>
> When you return to New York, do say goodbye to my sister for me, and thank her for her superb performance as Mrs Townsend . . .

> LEONARD
>
> I'll do that.

> VANDAMM
> (*gesturing towards Valerian*)
> . . . And you might tell your knife-throwing chum that I've reassured his wife.

> LEONARD
>
> Right.

*During this, Eve has been glancing about as though looking for a final means of escape. Her glance goes to Vandamm's hand still gripping her arm. She tries unsuccessfully to ease away from his grip. Leonard, seeing her actions, eases himself over to block any attempted escape she might be planning.*

> VANDAMM
>
> I guess that's all, Leonard.

*He starts to lead Eve towards the steps of the plane.*

> LEONARD
> (*looking at Eve*)
> Happy landing.

**CLOSE-UP: EVE**
*Panic begins to seize her. Suddenly, from the house, comes the sound of two quick gunshots.*

**THE GROUP**
*All turn their heads quickly.*

**POINT OF VIEW: FLASH**
*The flying figure of Thornhill is seen dashing out of the house and into the sedan parked outside.*

**THE GROUP**
*Still looking off. Suddenly Eve, finding herself momentarily free of Vandamm's grip and Leonard's observation, grabs the Tarascan warrior from Vandamm's arm and dashes out of the scene towards the house. Over this, we hear the distant car starting up. Leonard looks quickly at Vandamm for instructions.*

**VANDAMM**
*(sharply)*

Get that figure back!

*Leonard dashes away, with Valerian joining him.*

**REVERSE ANGLE**
*Eve is running a few paces ahead of the two men, the sedan speeding towards her. The car starts to pull up and its side door flies open as Eve reaches it.*

**SIDE-ON ANGLE**
*The car stops. Eve leaps in.*

**THORNHILL**
*(yells)*

Lock it!

*She slams the door just as the two men arrive. They tug at the handle. Thornhill guns the car away.*

**MEDIUM SHOT**
*The two men are flung back as the car drives off. It makes a wide circle and speeds towards the house over rough ground.*

INT. CAR

> EVE
> *(breathlessly)*
> What happened? Are you all right?

> THORNHILL
> Can you imagine? The housekeeper had me pinned down for
> five minutes before I realized it was that same silly gun of
> yours.

*He flashes a glance at the figure in her hands.*

> I see you got the . . . uh . . . pumpkin.

> EVE
> *(grimly)*
> Yes.

LANDING FIELD
*Vandamm has just reached the two men.*

> VALERIAN
> Don't worry, sir. The gates are locked.

AT THE GATES
*The car comes to a screeching stop before the locked gates. Thornhill
jumps out and starts tugging at the chains.*

CLOSE-UP: EVE IN CAR
*Still clutching the figure, she looks forward towards Thornhill anxiously,
then looks back.*

POINT OF VIEW
*With the house in the distance, she sees the running figures of Leonard
and Valerian.*

OBJECTIVE SHOT – THE CAR AND THE GATES
*Eve scrambles out of the car, runs towards Thornhill. He turns, sees the
men coming. Together, he and Eve run out of the shot.*

**LEONARD AND VALERIAN**
*Running after them.*

**INT. FOREST. DOLLY SHOT – MOONLIGHT**

*The 'forest' is really no more than a shallow, heavily wooded area. Thornhill and Eve come running in, and camera moves with them as they scramble over rocks, fallen trees and other obstacles. Eve is encumbered by her scarf, handbag and the figure she is carrying.*

**THORNHILL**
Here. Give me that.

*He takes the figure from her. They run on. Suddenly Eve is brought up short as the scarf around her neck gets caught on a pine tree. Thornhill stops, turns to her and they struggle to get her loose.*

**FLASH: LEONARD AND VALERIAN**
*Crashing through the forest after them.*

**THORNHILL AND EVE**
*Still trying to extricate her. Finally they unwind her from the scarf, abandon it and run out of shot.*

**LEONARD AND VALERIAN**
*Running after them.*

**LONG SHOT: EXTERIOR FOREST**
*In the distance, we see the running figures of Thornhill and Eve emerge from the forest into an open clearing. They continue towards camera until, in a close shot, they come to a sudden stop and look off ahead.*

**POINT OF VIEW**
*About fifty to a hundred yards ahead, they see the back of the Mt Rushmore monument. The heads of the presidents are moonlit. Beyond is yawning space, and beyond that, the distant horizon.*

**THORNHILL'S VOICE**
Uh oh. Didn't know you were here, gentlemen.

**STRAIGHT ON TWO SHOT: THORNHILL AND EVE**

**THORNHILL**
(*still looking ahead*)
No good this way. We're on top of the monument.

*He now looks off to his right and slightly behind him.*

**POINT OF VIEW**
*In the distance, Valerian is seen emerging from the forest.*

**CLOSE SHOT: THORNHILL AND EVE**
*Eve, looking off in another direction, grabs Thornhill's arm.*

**EVE**

Look!

*Thornhill looks off.*

**POINT OF VIEW**
*Leonard has emerged from the woods in another spot.*

**PROFILE SHOT: THORNHILL AND EVE**
*He grabs her arm and starts running with her in the only direction they can go – towards the edge of the monument. Camera dollies along with them until they start slowing down. Camera comes to a stop.*

**REVERSE ANGLE: FULL VIEW OF PART OF MONUMENT**
*We see the tiny figures of Thornhill and Eve approach the edge.*

**WAIST SHOT: THORNHILL AND EVE**
*As they peer down.*

**POINT OF VIEW**
*The presidents' faces as seen from the edge, with moonlight revealing the depth below.*

**WAIST SHOT: THORNHILL AND EVE**
*They turn, look back once more at their pursuers.*

187

THORNHILL
C'mon. Down we go.

EVE
*(looking down again)*
We can't.

THORNHILL
No choice. C'mon.

*They start down and go out of shot.*

LONG SHOT: CROSS ANGLE – THE MONUMENT
*Shooting past Lincoln's face in foreground, we see Thornhill and Eve
making their precarious way down the sloping crevice between
Jefferson's face and the rear of Washington's head.*

CLOSE ANGLE: THORNHILL AND EVE
*As they work their way down:*

THORNHILL
*(grimly)*
A funny thing happened to me the other day on my way to
the theatre.

EVE
What?

THORNHILL
Skip it.

COMPREHENSIVE SHOT OF LEONARD AND VALERIAN
*Still fairly far apart, arriving at the edge. Leonard is at the top of the
crevice. Valerian is on Washington's head.*

CLOSE ANGLE: THORNHILL AND EVE
*They look up and see:*

POINT OF VIEW
*Leonard starting down after them.*

**MEDIUM SHOT: THORNHILL AND EVE**
*Continuing their perilous descent down the slope.*

> THORNHILL
>
> If we get out of this alive, let's go back to New York on a train together. All right?

> EVE
>
> Is that a proposition?

> THORNHILL
>
> No – a proposal.

*He loses his footing, slips, dangles precariously. Eve reaches down, tries to help him.*

> EVE
>
> What happened to the first two marriages?

> THORNHILL
> *(struggling)*
>
> My wives divorced me.

> EVE
>
> Why?

> THORNHILL
> *(still struggling)*
>
> I think they . . . said I . . . led . . . too dull a life . . .

*He regains a safe foothold.*


**CLOSE SHOT: VALERIAN**
*Sliding rapidly down a sloping ledge to Washington's right shoulder and starting across.*


**LONG SHOT: CROSS ANGLE – THE MONUMENT**
*With Lincoln's nose and lips in foreground, we see Valerian making his way across beneath Washington's chin to head off Thornhill and Eve, who are coming down towards Washington's left shoulder with Leonard scrambling down after them.*

**HIGH ANGLE: LEONARD**
*Below him in background are Thornhill and Eve. Leonard accidentally dislodges a precariously balanced rock. It starts to tumble down the slope.*

**CLOSE SHOT: THORNHILL AND EVE**
*Their backs are to camera. They hear the rumbling rock, turn, eyes wide with dismay. There is no time for them to move out of the path of disaster.*

**POINT OF VIEW**
*The rock is crashing down towards camera. At the last moment, just as it is about to smash into its intended victims, the rock hits a snag and goes flying off at a tangent into the yawning depths below.*

**THORNHILL AND EVE**
*For a brief moment, stunned into immobility by their brush with death.*

> EVE
> *(in a hollow voice)*
> I just thought of a new drink . . .

> THORNHILL
> *(still staring ahead)*
> Really?

> EVE
> People, on-the-rocks.

*Thornhill gives her a look. She gives a little shrug. And then they quickly start down the ledge on Washington's left shoulder. (Right here, Eve's handbag, shoes and suit jacket become hopelessly encumbering. Thornhill makes her get rid of whatever she can. The shoes go flying away. So, too, the jacket, with womanly regrets. But Eve makes Thornhill stuff some of the contents of her handbag into his pockets before she hurls the handbag to the depths below. During this striptease, there should be some ad-libbed comments.) Preoccupied with their physical efforts, they are not aware of Valerian approaching in background. He gets closer and closer and now, with upraised knife, is about to stab Thornhill when Eve, turning suddenly, sees Valerian and shouts:*

Look out!

*Thornhill swings around, hits Valerian's wrist and deflects the downward arc of the knife in mid-air.* Then he quickly gives Eve the figure, *and shouts:*

THORNHILL

Keep going . . . !

*Eve moves on, with Leonard coming down after her, as Thornhill faces Valerian again.*

CLOSE ANGLE: THORNHILL AND VALERIAN
*Struggling to the death, with the knife poised between them in Valerian's hand.*

THORNHILL
(gasping)
I'm beginning . . . to think . . . you don't . . . *like* me . . .

*They wrestle each other to the ground, then roll over the edge and begin to slide down towards a precipitous drop, still struggling.*

**CLOSE SHOT: EVE**
*Looking back for a moment just as the two men start their slide. She turns away and scrambles on as she sees Leonard almost upon her.*

**THORNHILL AND VALERIAN**
*Still sliding down. At the very edge of the precipice, Thornhill manages to break free, and* the sudden release causes Valerian to plunge to his death with a terrible scream. *Thornhill gets to his feet, looks off, sees Leonard about to catch up with Eve. He starts towards them.*

**CLOSE ANGLE: EVE AND LEONARD**
*Leonard grabs Eve, wrests the figure from her grasp and gives her a vicious shove that sends her down to what appears to be certain death. But as she slips down, she manages to catch hold of a ridge in the precipitous slope and dangles there, unable to move.*

**ANOTHER ANGLE**
*As Thornhill arrives on the scene, Leonard is starting away with the figure. Thornhill clambers down to rescue Eve.*

**THORNHILL**

Hang on!

*He lowers himself down to Eve, placing himself in a perilous position. His only purchase is one hand gripping the edge above him while the other hand reaches out to take Eve's outstretched hand.*

**CLOSE SHOT: EVE**
*In her effort to reach Thornhill's hand, her feet apply pressure to the ridge she has been standing on. Just as their hands meet, the ridge breaks off and her legs dangle in mid-air.*

**OBJECTIVE SHOT**
*Thornhill, hanging on to the ledge above him with one hand, is holding Eve from death below with his other hand.*

**CLOSE SHOT: THORNHILL**
*Turning into camera with desperation to look over the ledge above him. He sees:*

**POINT OF VIEW**
*Leonard still moving away.*

**CLOSE SHOT: THORNHILL**

**THORNHILL**

Leonard!

**POINT OF VIEW: FROM THORNHILL**
*Leonard stops, turns and looks back.*

**THORNHILL'S VOICE**
*(off-screen)*

For God's sake . . .

*Leonard starts down towards him. As he approaches, the camera begins to pan down his body until suddenly Thornhill's hand appears in foreground gripping the ledge. The feet of Leonard slowly approach and come to a stop a few inches from the hand. Then one foot is raised and gently placed on the hand.*

**CLOSE-UP: THORNHILL**
*Glancing up sharply, reacting as he feels the pressure of the shoe on his fingers and realizes what is about to happen.*

**CLOSE-UP: LEONARD**
*Looking down without expression as he leans forward slightly and deliberately applies the full weight of his body on to the fingers.*

**CLOSE-UP: THORNHILL**
*In horrible agony.*

**THORNHILL**
*(gasps)*

Don't . . . . I . . . . can't . . .

*Eve cries out.*

**CLOSE-UP – SHOE PRESSED ON HAND**

> **THORNHILL'S VOICE**
> (*off-screen*)
>
> Have to . . . let . . . *go* . . .

*Suddenly there is the crack of a gun which reverberates through the monument. The shoe relaxes its pressure for a moment and the figure drops from Leonard's grasp to the ledge beside the hand and smashes,* revealing several rolls of microfilm.

**LONG SHOT: TOP OF THE MONUMENT**
*A brief flash of a group of silhouetted figures looking down.*

**CLOSE-UP: THORNHILL**
*Glancing briefly at the smashed figure and the microfilm, then looking up.*

**LOW ANGLE: LEONARD**
*Mortally wounded, looking down with dying eyes, then starting to fall towards camera.*

**THORNHILL AND EVE**
*Recoiling as Leonard's body falls past them.*

**LOW ANGLE: TOP OF MONUMENT**
*In a full figure shot, we see the group on the monument at close range: the Professor, holding a pair of binoculars; Vandamm, flanked by two uniformed State Troopers, one of whom is holding the revolver that fired the shot. Below them, two more State Police clamber down the slope to rescue Thornhill and Eve and disappear out of shot.*

> **PROFESSOR**
> (*staring down worriedly*)
>
> Well done, Sergeant.

> **VANDAMM**
> (*sardonically*)
>
> Rather unsporting, don't you think . . . using real bullets?

**CUT TO:**

**BIG HEAD CLOSE-UP: THORNHILL**
*Looking down with tension on his face.*

> **THORNHILL**
> (*with exertion*)
>
> Here . . . reach . . . *now* . . .

> **EVE'S VOICE**
> (*off-screen – gasping*)
>
> I'm . . . trying . . .

> **THORNHILL**
>
> Come on . . . I've got you . . . *up* . . .

**BIG HEAD CLOSE-UP: EVE**
*Looking up, her face showing physical effort.*

> **EVE**
>
> Can't make it –

> **THORNHILL'S VOICE**
> (*off-screen*)
>
> Yes you can . . . Come on . . .

> **EVE**
> (*strained*)
>
> Pull harder . . .

**BIG HEAD CLOSE-UP: THORNHILL**

> **THORNHILL**
>
> There . . . that's it . . .

**BIG HEAD CLOSE-UP: EVE**

> **EVE**
> (*moving up*)
>
> Ah . . . good . . .

*She starts to laugh.*

**MEDIUM SHOT: THORNHILL AND EVE**
*As she lands beside him, we realize that they are not on Mt Rushmore after all, but are sitting side by side, feet dangling from the upper berth of*

*a drawing-room in a train standing in a station at night. He has been lifting her up with difficulty because the lower berth is not open. From outside, a voice calls out: 'Board!'*

**EVE**
*(still laughing)*

This is silly, Thornhill.

**THORNHILL**

I know. But I'm sentimental.

*He puts his arms around her, and as they kiss lovingly, we see the hand that was stepped on. Each finger is neatly taped with a Band-Aid. Just then, the train jerks into motion.*

**EXT. TRAIN**

*We are shooting towards the rear of the observation car as the train rolls off into the night.*

**FADE OUT:**